MW00668186

Isn't That What We're Supposed to Believe?

Exploring Our Faith

by Don H. Alexander

Printed in the United States of America
Oklahoma City, Oklahoma
ISBN #1-885473-99-0

Scripture selections taken from The Revised Standard Version.

Produced by:

Pre-Production Press
2717 NW 50th
Oklahoma City, OK 73112
(405) 946-0621

Pre-Production Press is an imprint of
Wood 'N' Barnes Publishing & Distribution

Cover design by Judy Alexander

To order copies of this book, please call:
First Christian Church
3700 N. Walker
Oklahoma City, OK 73118
405-525-6551

Acknowledgments

✤ ✤   ✦ ✦

*Acknowledgment and thanks to Liz Burdette
for editing assistance with my final draft.*

*My appreciation to several friends who gave
an extra measure of encouragement in the
publishing of this book–
Ken & Sue White, Bob & Georgia Vaughn,
Earl & Madeline De Vilbiss, Frank Borglund and Colleen
Atlee.
I am also grateful to Jim & Mary K. Burmeier
and Jim & Gayle Larimore.*

*I appreciate the three-month sabbatical granted by
my church that allowed the unencumbered time for
undertaking this project.*

*And to my wife Judy, the light of my life,
who has kept my cup full to overflowing for more than 38
years, heartfelt thanks for her love and support.*

➜ Don Alexander

About the Author

Don H. Alexander has served as Senior Minister of the First Christian Church of Oklahoma City for the past 26 years.

He attended the University of Missouri briefly before returning to Oklahoma University where he received his B.A. degree in 1961. Dr. Alexander received two graduate degrees from Yale University Divinity School and in 1996 was awarded the honorary Doctor of Divinity Degree from Phillips Theological Seminary.

In 1979 Dr. Alexander hosted his own religious television series entitled, "Where the People Are," and the following year First Christian joined with Presbyterian and Methodist churches in presenting "Oklahoma City at Worship."

Dr. Alexander has been an adjunct professor of preaching at Phillips Seminary and is well known for his insightful and flavorful invocations. He has lectured, preached and prayed for numerous civic and denominational gatherings. Having shared the podium with Charleton Heston at a men's dinner group, Mr. Heston remarked he had never heard an invocation applauded before that evening!

First Christian Church served as the family disaster relief center following the bombing of the Alfred P. Murrah Building in April of 1995. For three weeks, more than 500 people a day were fed, nurtured, counseled and housed, when necessary, in the church facility.

Relating to the tragedy, Dr. Alexander held numerous radio, television and newsprint interviews, including Larry King Live, Oprah Winfrey Show, CNN News, French television stations, Christian Science Monitor and BBC, seeking to speak a sane word in the midst of chaos, saying repeatedly, "A moment of insanity should not be allowed to define our humanity," and "God's heart was the first to break when the bomb exploded!" Letters from across the world thanked this church and this clergyman for speaking a helpful and hopeful word in response to such a terrible tragedy.

Dr. Alexander is a member of the advisory board of the Disaster Memorial Committee and his first sermon in response to the bombing, "Words, Words, Words,–the Enduring Gift" was published in "And the Angels Wept."

Don and his wife Judy have two grown children: a son Eric and his wife Star, a daughter and son-in-law, AnnLynn and Steve Buchanan and two outstanding grandchildren, Haley and Alex Buchanan! They have a remote mountain retreat the family built themselves where Don is able to devote time and energy to devotional study and writing. He is currently working on two other books he hopes to complete in the near future.

Preface

Once upon a time several serious minded religious thinkers were discussing the question of ultimate authority. They quizzed one another about their foundational beliefs. Where does one turn for the final word? What, they asked each other, is your ultimate authority?

Several denominations were represented. The Presbyterian said that John Calvin was his ultimate authority. The Methodist said she guessed her ultimate authority would be John Wesley. The Catholic said the Pope. The Baptist said the Bible. Then they all turned to the person from the Christian Church (Disciples of Christ) and asked, "What is your ultimate authority?" He smiled thoughtfully and replied, "Well, it seems to me..."

Now I like that response, and I do not believe it is shallow or ill considered. Nor is it self-centered or egotistical. Because what I mean when I make such a response is, *after full consideration of a number of factors, then it seems to me.*

And what are those factors? They are a thorough grounding in the Biblical story, attention to the teachings of the best thinkers over the centuries, knowledge of advances in literary and scientific thought, seeking the leading of God's spirit in the task of interpretation and the application of personal experience and reason to all of the above.

When all of these factors have been considered, then a person may say with responsibility and seriousness, "Well, it seems to me."

This, then, provides a sense of context for all that is to follow. I will be saying *how it seems to me* as we explore together the purpose of religion, the authority of the Bible, language about God and prayer and how Jesus can be talked about in ways that make sense for the next century.

I invite you to join me in the quest!

This book has been in gestation for the past seven years. In the spring of 1991 I read Thomas Oden's *Agenda for Theology*, and it reawakened some of the objections that I have felt since seminary days about certain Christological assumptions that few seem to question.

That Jesus is God according to Nicea (325 A.D.), that the early church fathers seem to have gone against "the sense of the scriptures" in their Christological conclusions, that the church has generally accepted conciliar formulas over Biblical images, that we seemed "stuck" with a supernatural metaphysics for the last 1500 years, that "orthodoxy" has been understood as fixed and static–these are the kinds of assumptions that I have seen affirmed in various arenas and in Oden's book in particular. These views are not reflective of my own thinking or that of many of my ministerial colleagues.

A heart attack and bypass surgery in 1992 interrupted the process. But in 1994 I presented a brief "Christological overview" to a district ministers' gathering in Oklahoma City which provided the outline that grew into this book.

Then in April of 1995, Oklahoma City experienced the awful tragedy of the Murrah Building bombing. The response of our city was heroic, deeply compassionate and highly professional.

Comparisons were drawn with other tragedies and some talked about "the Oklahoma standard," noting that there was no looting and that so many volunteered so willingly.

When goods such as boots, gloves and food stuffs were needed, they were delivered almost immediately by the truckload, always brand new and, in almost every situation, donated.

The outpouring of human caring was indeed, magnificent. *Yet*, in the midst of the tragedy and the heroic response, some things were said, in the desire to comfort and explain, that made God sound very capricious and manipulative.

Some articles and books were published and some words were spoken in media interviews that made it seem that God had been active in letting some live while allowing others to die. These kinds of statements surfaced theological concerns that were not unrelated to the often inaccurate and misleading ways in which we talk about Jesus and how Jesus is related to God.

So the scope of my endeavor enlarged. It is not possible to talk about Christology in a vacuum. How we read and understand the Bible and how we think about God–these have their consequences in how we think about Jesus as the Christ.

How we think and talk about God and Jesus will have consequences in how we understand suffering and how and why we engage in prayer. And all of these bear on our religious life–why we do and think and act in the ways that we do.

This book, then, in a sense shaped itself. It seemed that it would be helpful to talk about the purpose of religion and how we understand the Bible *as a context* for wrestling with issues of theological concern such as God, Jesus, the messianic hope, human suffering and prayer.

For instance, did Jesus have to die on the cross as part of some foreordained drama?

How can that kind of question even be approached without first seeking some common ground in terms of how we understand the Bible, how God and Jesus are related and how Jesus' presence in the world may have saving power?

I have been in active ministry for more than three decades and for the past 26 years have served as the senior minister of the First Christian Church of Oklahoma City, Oklahoma. The members are a loving, supportive and questing congregation. They should not, however, be held responsible for the theological or Christological views expressed in the following pages.

Some of my own church family may not agree with my conclusions, but in the Christian Church (Disciples of Christ) we have agreed to disagree agreeably, or more importantly, to respect one another in the process of dialogue.

This book is by no means conclusive. I mean it to be suggestive, not exhaustive, and I hope it will inspire further dialogue.

Contents

✦ Don Alexander

Introduction

Christology is the study of what Jesus Christ means for us and for the world. The Greek word for "Messiah" is "Christos," which suggests the derivation of the term "Christology." But Christology is more than just a study of the "Messianic expectation" and whether Jesus fulfilled that expectation or transformed it. Christology also asks about the other titles for Jesus used in the New Testament and deals with how Jesus is related to God.

Is Jesus divine? The word "divine" bears very broad definition. Many would say that there are *divine* elements in our humanity. Is Jesus "the same as God" or "distinct from God"? Is Jesus Christ "the Godman" or "God's man"? That is the essential question addressed in this study. Christology is not a word we hear often; but, for the Christian, it should be the first major subheading under "Theology."

I do not know who will read this book. Will it be students assigned certain passages as part of an introductory course in theology? Will it be individuals in an adult Sunday school class looking for some new perspective about what God is like? Will it be preachers hoping to break out of faith traditions that discourage the interpretive process and thus the possibility of new insights?

Whatever the motive of the reader I am convinced that the breath of God, the wind of God's spirit, is an ever-freshening reality, and that it will be to our own detriment and the dishonoring of God if we fail to reexamine our belief systems with regularity and with intensity. That is what this book is about.

Certainly there is a kind of "caughtness" about all theological endeavor. Every generation is "caught" (sometimes "trapped")

1

by its own world-view—that is, how we've been taught to look at the world. Our own life experiences (interpreted by our world-view), how much we've been influenced (or not influenced) by the arts, literature, science and mythologies of our own and previous times, how much we have been taught to respect and/or challenge authority—all of these and more will bear on our theological leanings.

1)   Several pitfalls to theological thinking can be described: sometimes, for instance, whole generations of people can be "caught" by the phrase (or the subconsciously communicated idea), "but that's what we're supposed to believe."

Several years ago a well-read, thoughtful Presbyterian minister friend said to me, "Don, there hasn't been any significant new approach to Christology in the last 1500 years. We are still parroting the same old stuff without really examining what it means."

What he was saying was that generations of people had been caught and trapped by the fear that there could be no deviation from "what we're supposed to believe." Consequently, we continue to talk about Christology (what Christ means) in terms that, in some measure, no longer carry meaning in our common language for our own time.

Actually, of course, quite a bit has been done in Christology over the last 1500 years; but, for the most part, it has not arrived at the door of the church or the pastor's study. It has remained in the academy — a conversation between colleagues rather than a word to the church. This brief study is intended for public consumption, to address the pastor and the church with a Christology that makes sense for our time.

2)   A second phrase sometimes still heard in religious dialogue is, "Well, it does not matter what you believe, just so you believe

in something." Surely allegiance to that kind of sentiment reduces the whole religious enterprise to no more than a game of Monopoly and has absolutely no meaning in terms of real daily living. Oh, we jostle back and forth in competitive maneuvering to see who will get Boardwalk or Park Place; but, when the evening's fun is over, it really does not matter a whit.

It is, of course, my conviction that what we believe matters tremendously. What we believe will determine what we become, what we will do with our lives, and how we will treat others. It is far more than just an evening's entertainment.

The recent popularity of books such as William Bennett's *Book of Virtues* and Dr. Laura Schlesinger's *How Could You Do That* are clear illustrations that a large segment of our society is, in fact, almost desperate for something in which to believe. We feel compelled to rekindle the values that can focus the direction of our lives and of our children's lives.

3)   A third common pitfall is simply lack of knowledge, the failure to assimilate the stories of faith as found in the Jewish and Christian scriptures–failure, that is, to know the Bible in some fullness of dimension.

Some of our current Christological perspective is not so much the result of wrestling with the multi-faceted perspectives provided in the New Testament. It is with the continued acceptance of the interpretations of the early church councils without subjecting them to rigorous review. And this review should be in the light of what the Bible itself has to say.

We must know the Bible and Bible stories, the soil out of which faith grows. And then we must not be afraid to engage the text through dialogue and interpretation.

A minister once walked into a children's Sunday school class

3

while the lesson was in progress and asked the question, "Who broke down the walls of Jericho?" One little boy answered, "It wasn't me, sir." The preacher turned to the teacher and asked, "Is this the usual behavior in this class?" The teacher answered, "This boy is honest, and I believe him if he said he didn't do it."

Leaving the room the preacher sought an elder and explained what had happened. The elder said, "I have known both the boy and the teacher for many years, and I'm sure the lad didn't do it."

By this time the preacher was heartsick and reported to the Department of Christian Education. They said, "We see no point in being so upset. Let's pay the bill for the damage to the walls and charge it to upkeep."

Not knowing the tradition, they completely misunderstood the preacher's question and could not imagine that it might hold some meaning for them.

This is the second part of the equation. It isn't just a matter of knowing the material. It is also very much a matter of developing the spiritual capacity to do something with the material. In his book *Overhearing the Gospel* Dr. Fred Craddock says, "There is an understanding peculiar to the righteous man, to the person who lives within an understanding distance of God" (p. 36).

Surely that is the goal of all our endeavor—"to come within an understanding distance of God." In the final analysis the purpose of Bible study, of all religious dialogue, of this book, is to explore and find out more about what God is like and what, by God's help, we may become.

In terms of Christology we must know our traditions and, most importantly, what the Bible says about Jesus—who he is, how he is related to God and how he understood himself and his mission. We must know the stories and then take the further step—we must

4

engage in interpretive dialogue, seeking the meaning of those stories for our own time in such a way that our spiritual capacity will increase.

When we short-circuit either part of the process, knowing the material *or* interpreting what it means for us, we do a monumental disservice to self and to God.

For 1500 years the church has tended to be one-dimensional as to what the Bible says about Christ–more focused on what the "Church Fathers" (early Catholic Bishops) have said (what "we're supposed to believe") than on the Biblical narrative itself. It has been content just to keep paying the bills and charging it to up-keep, rather than reviewing and renewing the story and seeking its relevance for human life today.

In the pages that follow I hope to honor both parts of the process: knowing the story *and* interpreting it for contemporary humanity.

We do not live in 500 A.D., and the language framework and the world-view of that time are not adequate or appropriate for the 21st century. Neither do we live in the first century, and the interpretive process must take cognizance of that as well. Still we are indebted to what has gone before and will dialogue with it with respect and appreciation for the cultural forces that moved in those times. My intent is to set context and direction for continuing dialogue.

This will be a suggestive rather than an exhaustive study of the Christological problems. I hope its content will stimulate further quest on the part of the reader.

The questions raised at the beginning of chapters 1 and 2 are meant to be provocative. They may not *all* be specifically answered in the course of this book, but asking meaningful questions can be a part of orthodoxy, that is, "right teaching." This was not foreign to Jesus' approach–for instance: "Why do you call me good?" (Mark 10:18), and "Which of these, do you think, proved neighbor to the man who fell among robbers?" (Luke 10:36).

✦ ✦   ✦   ✦

1

When Religion is Wrong...

This is a book primarily about Christology. What do we believe about Jesus Christ? What is the meaning of his life? How does what we believe about him complement, add to or detract from what we believe about God? Is our Christology dependent on our theology, or is our theology dependent on our Christology?

Does what we say we believe about Jesus seem at times to stand in direct contradiction to what we affirm to be the larger purposes of God? Does our Christology tend to be inclusive or exclusive? Is it confessional or authoritarian and coercive? What has the dogma of the church affirmed in centuries past, and what should be the emphasis for the next century?

These are the kind of questions with which we will be dealing within the context of careful attention to the scriptures. We will be much more concerned with the Biblical witness than with the postulations of the early church fathers — though both will be considered.

But, first, some setting of the stage, some providing of context out of which, and for the sake of which, the Christological questions must be raised.

The broad context is that of religion. The Latin root of the word is the same as "ligament" — that which binds, connects or holds together. The fundamental human longing is for God. As Augustine said, "Our hearts are restless until they find their rest in thee." The function of religion is to reconnect us with God, to help us find our rest in the divine, to hold us together with that which can give meaning and shape to life, that which can give life in fullest dimension.

The more immediate context is that of religion in America today. Is religion fulfilling its stated purpose? The answer is, of course, mixed–yes and no and some maybes in between.

There are those for whom religion is the defining center of their lives, continually reconnecting them with that which gives life in fullest dimension. But there are countless others for whom religion has become either a matter of idolatry—making an idol out of some guru-type, ego-centered personality or worshipping a theological perspective that is demeaning to both God and humanity—or, simply superficial, that is, only skin-deep and not touching the heart of life.

There is a child's nursery rhyme that says,

> *"There was a little girl and she had a little curl*
> *Right in the middle of her forehead.*
> *When she was good, she was very, very good,*
> *But when she was bad, she was horrid."*

Religion is a lot like that little girl. When it is good, it is very, very good—but, when it is bad, it is horrid.

In the religious arena we do not want to be quarrelsome. We want our demeanor, our behavior toward those of differing points of view to somehow recommend us even to those with whom we disagree. Surely we want to underscore the common ground, the great positives that bind us to one another and to our God, and not the negatives that divide us. But religion-gone-wrong has received so much press in the last couple of decades that for the sake of clarification and edification some evaluation is needed.

The perverted use of religion is wrong. Vulnerable people have been drawn to cults that led them to mass suicide. Televangelists have practiced unethical fund raising tactics. Faith healers have preyed on the piety and gullibility of sincere people hungry for help. We have failed to address the issue of birth control on a worldwide scale at least partially because of the continuing authoritarian stance of one major arm of the Christian tradition. Theological fuzziness in various branches of the church has encouraged a kind of magical approach to religion.

These kinds of realities require comment. Religious expression can be wrong; and when it is, it ought to be addressed.

Certainly Jesus addressed it. He challenged the Pharisees at every turn when he perceived that their religious expression was leading the people away from God, when he perceived that their religion was wrong.

1)   Religion is wrong when it tempts us to set ourselves up as superior to others, or when it is too success-oriented, has too much gloss and glitter, and is out of touch with the issues of daily living.

Such an attitude stunts spiritual growth and stifles sensitivity to the needs of others. For instance, remember the prayer of the self-righteous Pharisee, "God, I thank thee that I am not like other men . . ." (Luke 18:11). But he was like other men and so are we all—struggling, imperfect, weak, needing all the help we can get. Any religion that encourages us to forget our own vulnerability is wrong.

The real tragedy is not that some television preachers did things they should have been ashamed of, but that so much money and television time were spent portraying an image that was a false assumption of a religious appearance. And that needs to be acknowledged. As we shall see, the pitfall of hypocrisy is sometimes present in Christological formulations.

2)   The second way in which religion can be wrong is closely related to the first; that is, when the emphasis is on form rather than substance. Emphasis on right form rather than right action makes the container more important than the contents. There is a sense in which *how* we believe (the actions of faith) may be more important than *what* we believe (doctrine—form or formulas rather than substance).

Perhaps we should put more emphasis on the manner (or manners) of our faithfulness than on the object of our faith. Jesus' contention with the Pharisees was not over the object of their faith but the legalistic, judgmental manner of their faithfulness. Jesus was addressing this very issue when he said, "Not everyone who says to me, 'Lord, Lord,' shall enter the kingdom of heaven, but he who does the will of my Father who is in heaven" (Matthew 7:21). The emphasis here is not on the object of faith but on the manner of one's faithfulness. Form should not deny substance.

The Pharisees knew about proper form—how to wash one's hands, how to purify oneself for worship, how to pray, work, walk, study. If the form was right, that was what counted. However, Jesus said, "these you ought to have done without neglecting the others" (justice, mercy and faith) (Matthew 23:23).

This brief note recently appeared in the *Wall Street Journal*: "The elms in South Park, Pa., must be cut down because they are obstructing the monument to Joyce Kilmer. They have lifted their leafy arms so high that the passersby can no longer read the inscription which begins, 'I think that I shall never see a poem lovely as a tree.'"

Perhaps we all need to examine our lives to see how vulnerable we are to sacrificing the trees (true value or substance) to superficial considerations. In the final analysis, of course, form and substance really cannot be separated. How we live (that is, the manner of our faithfulness) is very likely to be a direct reflection of what, in fact, we believe about God.

For instance, some Shiite Moslems gravely misunderstand the purposes of God in our world. If they knew God better, violence could not be their lodestar.

If those early Salem Christians had known God better, there would have been no hanging of innocent women as witches.

What fired the Crusades was an ugly misunderstanding of what God is like.

One thing follows another. There is a cause-effect relationship between what we really believe about God and how we live.

And so I ask, "What kind of God is this? What is the essential nature of the God we worship?"

When our religion does not produce a coherence between form and substance, it is wrong. Again and again in Matthew 23, Jesus addresses the scribes and the Pharisees as *actors*. Our Bible translators used the word "hypocrite" which literally means "playing a role."

3) Religious expression that preys on ignorance and superstition is wrong. Why? Because religion that portrays God as less than human is wrong. That is what Jesus' driving the money changers out of the temple was all about. It angered Jesus to see commercial advantage being taken from the piety of sincere worshipers.

Several years ago a young woman was photographed in a church parking lot in Texas carrying a placard that read, "God is not a blackmailer." That girl was more in tune with God's voice than the televangelist who said, "God would call him home" if he didn't raise $8 million by a certain date. That evangelist may have heard something, but surely it was not God. He may have been sincere, but it is possible to be sincerely wrong. To justify shabby, deceitful methods of fundraising in the service of God is very much a disservice to and a dishonoring of God.

I may not know exactly what God sounds like, but I do know what God does not sound like. I certainly do not know everything God will say, but I do know certain things God will not say. How do I know? Because the Bible and clear thinking and the best in the human journey tell me so. (I'll deal more explicitly with this "knowing" in a later chapter.)

But suffice it here to say that healthy, religious expression will not encourage the superstitious manipulation of God — whether through monetary gifts to the right guru, adherence to doctrines that fly in the face of well-grounded scientific knowledge and widely accepted advances in Biblical studies, or the incantation of certain creeds or liturgical phrases as being the only *right* words. Such expressions tend to mire the religious enterprise in the quicksand of *easy* answers and unexamined thought processes.

In *Violence Unveiled* Gil Bailie asserts, "There may be no more urgent task today than that of renouncing religious superstition" (p. 12). However, he cautions that we are not likely to do that by abandoning the spiritual tradition (Jewish/Christian) that taught us to be wary of religious superstition in the first place.

His affirmation is that the Hebrew prophets and the New Testament "represent the world's mother lode of anti-superstition" (p. 13).

Remember, it was Isaiah who announced God's disapproval of evil living wrapped in the camouflage of religious ritual. "I cannot endure iniquity and solemn assembly. Your new moons and your appointed feasts my soul hates; they have become a burden to me, I am weary of bearing them" (Isaiah 1:13-14).

And it was Jesus who said that we were to worship God with "heart . . . soul . . . and . . . MIND" (Matthew 22:37).

4)   Finally, religion that discourages personal accountability and responsibility—encouraging us to believe that God or some guru or T.V. evangelist, or your local church preacher or priest will do for us those things which we can and should do for ourselves—is wrong.

As *consumers* we have the continuing responsibility of discriminating between hucksterism, the possibly distorted ego needs of the speaker, and the true word of God.

We want our religious expressions to be appropriate, to do honor to God's name, to bring greater health and wholeness and compassion to the human endeavor. We want clarity of vision and honesty of spirit so that we do not distort the words of life. We want to be kind and caring, rightly dividing the word of truth.

But to do these things we must put ourselves in the arena, taking the first step toward responsible religion, learning about our faith. This means paying attention to content, getting to know the Bible and church tradition and immersing ourselves in the interpretive process; that is, relating the words of faith to our own experience of life.

In a 1993 speech at the Oklahoma Christian University of Science and Arts, George Gallup, Jr. said that there was an appalling lack of knowledge about the Bible among American Christians. He suggested that a skin-deep faith is responsible for much of the acrimony among Christians. He charged that most American believers are "cultural Christians" practicing a watered-down version of Christianity that leads to argument and intolerance.

"The historic fact," he said, "is that most Americans don't know what they believe or why. . . . Most of us would be hard pressed to defend our faith."

Gallup drew the logical conclusion that it is "flabby spirituality" that makes us "highly vulnerable to counterfeit religions that glorify self and not God. . . . So there's an awful lot of work to be done about informing people about their own faith. Really, the first task is to Christianize those in the pews."

In his concluding remarks Gallup made two complementary statements, one negative and one positive. He said that only about 13 percent of Americans are "highly spiritually committed." And then he said that contrary to conventional wisdom, the deeper individuals go into their faith the more open they become; and that these "hidden saints," as Gallup referred to them, are twice as likely to be involved in charitable activities and are also much happier than the rest of the population.

It sounds like a sermon outline–more open, more charitable and happier people. I have not preached it yet, but surely I will.

The implication is fairly obvious. Those who *know* (head knowledge and heart knowledge) their faith best; that is, the 13 percent who have a deeper level of spiritual commitment, are the ones who are experiencing life in fullest dimension. They have meaning and shape to their existence. Their religion is doing for them what it should do when it is more than skin-deep.

What about the other 87 percent? Some, of course, practice no religion in any conscious manner. They are the disaffected. Some fall under Gallup's "skin-deep, watered-down, cultural Christians" category. And some are deeply immersed in a kind of religion that misses the mark or, in the simple phrasing of the nursery rhyme, is *bad* and *horrid*.

This book is framed under a *shot-gun* metaphor. I am hoping to address the *broad field*. For the highly spiritually committed there may be the satisfaction of the ongoing quest, going deeper through the continuing interpretive process. We are all still journeying, and it can be fun once in awhile to turn corners and run into some sense of "shared journey," some "aha's!" that give a sense of reconnecting to each other and to our God.

It is also my hope that the disaffected, those not consciously aware of any religion in their lives, might feel addressed by more *common sense* (less supernatural and less superstitious) Christological categories and consider anew the viability of Christianity for their own lives.

For those who are only superficially Christian (who would admit such a thing?) it may be that the following chapters on nuancing our language about God, responsible Biblical interpretation, the purpose of prayer, and ways in which we can speak more meaningfully about Jesus Christ (how he can reveal more effectively to us the heart of God) will have a deepening effect in terms of personal faith.

For those who are caught in a religion that is partly or mostly *wrong,* in the sense of not making life more meaningful, more satisfying, more loving and more open to others, I urge you especially to stay with me through this endeavor. It is my deepest conviction that Jesus of Nazareth, a real historical figure, is the Christ, God's man for those who would follow him into a more meaningful relationship with the Creator, Judge and Redeemer of life. He is also the Son of the living God, a special relationship with God which he invites us to share that we might also enter the kingdom, and he can be called the savior of life (mine, yours and the world's).

By this I mean that a *right* understanding and application of Jesus' life, message and mission can "save us from all ills in this world and the next." Not in the sense of removing them, the "ills" (the evil, the wrong and the hurtful are there and must be confronted and dealt with) but in the sense of "empowering us," giving us the capacity to deal with them because we are experiencing "Emmanuel"–God with us.

By *right* understanding I do not mean "correctness of belief," as in holding firm to certain doctrinal views; I mean to emphasize here more of "a relationship with." It is the point Marcus Borg is making under the heading "Beyond Belief to Relationship" in his book, *Meeting Jesus Again for the First Time.*

> "The experiences of my mid-thirties led me to realize that God is, and that the central issue of the Christian life is not believing in God or believing in the Bible or believing in the Christian tradition. Rather, the Christian life is about entering into a relationship with that to which the Christian tradition points, which may be spoken of as God, the risen living Christ, or the Spirit. And a Christian is one who lives out his or her relationship to God within the framework of the Christian tradition" (p. 17).

Too often we have operated from confused definitions about the meaning of *faith*. Faith is not the uncritical acceptance of the patently unbelievable, but living by the best that we can know.

To live by an outmoded belief is to be trapped in a superstitious approach to life. There was a time when a "flat-world" theory was an article of faith. And it served a good purpose. It kept seafarers from journeying too far out on the ocean in inadequate vessels.

But technological and scientific advances brought safer ships and a broader, sounder vision of the world on which we live.

To live by the "best that we can know" in navigational parlance today is light years removed from the experiences of the Apostle Paul in sailing the Mediterranean in his time.

So what is faith? Believing and trusting that certain characteristics are what God is like and living by them in our time and place.

Christian faith is not the unquestioning belief in certain details of the Jesus story such as virgin birth, a specific formula for baptism or magically moving mountains. Rather, Christian faith says that the message and mission of Jesus' living give greater clarity to what God is like and therefore to what God wants us to become.

The goal of our faith is not to enshrine virginity or to make certain rituals obligatory for entrance into the kingdom or to undermine the natural order of things by moving mountains with magic rather than by effort.

Jesus' image of "moving a mountain into the sea" was never meant to be taken literally anymore than when you tell a co-worker, "I've got a ton of work to do today." Both are figures of speech.

Jesus meant, "a little faith goes a long way" or "with even a little faith you can do great things."

Remember, faith does not mean holding certain doctrines as inviolate but living in the light of certain convictions about the character and purposes of God.

Faith is saying, here is what God is like and so here is how we should live. It is not a matter of believing certain doctrines but having a trusting relationship with God.

Religiously speaking, the "best that we can know," I believe, finds its definition in God. And, for Christians, God's being is clarified through our relationship to Jesus Christ and our under-standing of how God and Jesus are related. But this must be interpreted and expressed in the language and world-view of our own day.

One final clarification will be dealt with more fully in the last chapter dealing with Christological directions for the 21st century. When I make my personal affirmation of faith in Jesus as the Christ, the Son of the living God and Savior, it is neither a coercive nor an exclusive statement. For instance, when in 2 Corinthians 5:19 Paul says that "God was in Christ reconciling the world to himself," he does not say that God was ONLY in Christ.

In conclusion, then, *good* religion will be healthy-minded and healthy-hearted. It will create a healthier framework for facing and experiencing life.

Religion at its best will reconnect us to God and to our fellow human beings in ways that are life-giving and life-affirming. It will make the Bible more comprehensible, God more accessible, praying less mysterious and Jesus more human and more real.

So what about the Bible? How important is it to our religious journey?

◈ When Religion is Wrong... ◈
Chapter One Questions for Study and Discussion

1. What is the purpose of religion?

2. Martin Luther said, "Whatever your heart clings to and relies upon, that properly is your God." What do our hearts "cling to and rely upon?"

3. Is it possible to dishonor God? If so, how?

4. Can you think of some examples when religion has done more harm than good?

→ Don Alexander

2

What About the Bible?

We are coming to the Christological questions: How did Jesus understand himself? How self-aware was he in his sense of mission? Is it necessary to claim divinity for Jesus? Did he claim it for himself? Does it matter one way or another in our presentation of Jesus to the contemporary world? We shall address these questions–but not quite yet.

Our primary source for responding to such questions will be the Biblical record. What does the Bible say? That will be paramount in our quest. Of course we will look briefly at the tradition of the church's teaching (the church's interpretation over the centuries as conveyed, for instance, in the writings of Thomas Oden and Raymond Brown), but the Biblical emphasis will be our primary concern.

We will also do some interpreting of our own as we bring personal experience, the reality of cultural diversities, an analytical approach and our contemporary world-view (how we perceive the world in our modern technological age) to our search. Most importantly, we will seek God's energy to lead us through some of these channels toward a better understanding of the Biblical message.

However, before dealing with the Christological questions we continue to set the stage for our inquiry by asking the question, "What about the Bible?"

Sometimes it can be helpful, for the sake of clarification, to say what an object or concept is *not* before proceeding to its more positive definitions.

1)   The Bible is not God. Surely, most would say, that is self-evident and does not need stating, but some in the Christian community have at times seemed to deify the Bible, by claiming for the Bible power and authority that properly belong only to God. This has been called "bibliolatry"–making an idol, a God-image, out of the Bible.

Phrases like "The Bible said it. I believe it and that settles it" not only tend toward the idolatrous, but also betray a lack of acquaintance with the breadth and scope of the Biblical text itself.

For instance, compare the genealogies for Jesus in Matthew 1 and in Luke 3. They cannot be reconciled. But that is not needed if we recognize that these two authors have different agendas in mind and use their genealogical listings for their own particular purposes.

Matthew wants to associate Jesus with the *chosen* of God, the children of the promise, and so traces Jesus' lineage back to Abraham. Luke's genealogy, on the other hand, begins with Adam, establishing Jesus' place in the whole human family. This is consistent with Luke's stronger appeal to a Gentile audience and his emphasis on the universality of Christ's message.

In Matthew's listing there are supposedly three sets of 14 generations between Abraham and Jesus, which would make 42 generations, but the count is short one in both the first and third sets. In Luke's genealogy there are 56 generations listed between Abraham and Jesus.

Bishop John Spong sums up this issue quite succinctly in his book *Born of a Woman*, "Surely inerrancy is a virtue ascribed to the Bible only by those who do not bother to read great sections of Holy Writ" (p. 69).

My point is simply to illustrate the human factor in the production of the scriptures. The Bible is not literally factual in every detail, and the Bible is not God.

Actually the Bible suggests a perspective within which to understand the Bible. The first commandment in Exodus 20:3 says, "You shall have no other gods before me." A god is whatever we regard as ultimate and transcendent (the final authority), and we are not to treat any finite, relative, eminent entity (not even the Bible) as if it were the final authority, or divine.

2)   The Bible is not one-dimensional and was not meant to be read literalistically. The whole spirit of Jesus and the prophets seems to have been to liberate people from a literalistic/legalistic approach so they would indeed be free to live out the claims of God's love in the emerging realities of their own experiences.

By his own example Jesus invites us to interpret and to seek the leading of God's spirit that lies behind the words. And so he could say in Matthew 5:21, 27, 31, 33, 38 and 43, "You have heard that it was said . . . but I say to you . . ." and thus repeatedly put the emphasis, not on the letter of the law (which as Paul said in 2 Corinthians 3:6 "kills"), but on the spirit ("which makes alive," 2 Corinthians 3:6). He was *interpreting* the scriptures of his own day.

When I say that the Bible is not one-dimensional, I mean that it has many dimensions and much variety. It can be seen in startling incidences to be self-contradictory or at least in dialogue with itself. That is, *the Bible offers differing points of view on the same subject.* It is complex rather than simple. Often it seems to contain more paradoxy than orthodoxy.

By way of illustration: In Matthew 3:13-17 and in Mark 1:9-11 the writers are clear that John baptized Jesus, but in Luke 3:18-22 it is equally clear that John could not baptize Jesus because John was already in prison. The purpose in pointing this out is not to destroy faith but to help us understand how the Bible came into being piecemeal, with different authors who had different agendas.

"The critic," as Ronald Allen affirmed in his fine article in the Summer 1993 issue of "Biblical Literacy Today" helps us ask, "Why do Matthew and Mark have it one way while Luke has it another way? And does this difference affect our trust in the living God?"

Or what about issues such as Christ's return (popularly referred to as "the second coming"), divorce, slavery or homosexuality? On none of these issues is the Bible one-dimensional.

We can sometimes see a kind of chronological development. Dealing with Christ's return or the end of time, for instance, we read in Mark 9:1 these words of Jesus, "Truly, I say to you, there are some standing here who will not taste death before they see the kingdom of God come with power. "Sounds pretty imminent. But remember Mark's was the earliest of the gospels written (60-65 A.D.).

What happens, though, when several generations come and go, Jesus has not returned, and the kingdom has not come (at least not in terms of any ordinary measurements)? And so we turn to 2 Peter 3:8-9. Most biblical scholars today date 2 Peter, written around 125 A.D., as one of the latest books in the New Testament.

Here we read a kind of pastoral rationalization to those who are having trouble dealing with the fact that grandparents and parents have died, and Jesus still has not come. "But do not ignore this one fact, beloved, that with the Lord one day is as a thousand years and a thousand years as one day. The Lord is not slow about his promise as some count slowness, but is forbearing toward you, not wishing that any should perish, but that all should reach repentance." The Bible is interpreting itself, speaking a different word for a different moment in time.

A markedly contrasting approach to the "end time" can be seen in the treatment in John's Gospel, John 5:24. "Truly, truly, I say to you, he who hears my word and believes him who sent me, has eternal life. He does not come into judgment, but has passed from death to life."

Here there is no need to wait for Jesus' return. Hearing Jesus' word and believing God has already brought eternal life. It is a present possession. Some have called this "realized eschatology." The eschaton (end time) is already present in the person of Jesus. He will not have to come back; he is already here. This is a different interpretation from that of either Mark or 2 Peter.

It is also interesting when we can see two different levels of thought illustrated in the pronouncements of one author. In Romans 1:26, Paul reflects his cultural/religious bias against homosexuality, and yet in Galatians 3:28, he proclaims the larger spiritual vision that "There is neither Jew nor Greek, there is neither slave nor free, there is neither male nor female; for you are all one in Christ Jesus." Here he seems to be saying that in Christ all distinctions fall away, whether those distinctions be racial, cultural or sexual. It is certainly a different kind of approach and a different point of view from the Romans' passage.

3)   And it should be said that the Bible was not meant to be used as a battering-ram to condemn others, but rather more as a mirror for self-reflection.

The April 1993 issue of *"The Disciple,"* the primary journal of my own denomination, the Christian Church (Disciples of Christ), contained this helpful reminder from the editors with accompanying illustrations:

> "We must ever remember that the Bible is a book which encourages us to measure ourselves, not someone else.
>
> What brought Jesus to the cross was not the machinations of a particular race or nationality. God's intention is not to condemn Pharisees but legalism that has lost its concern for people. Not to condemn Jews but a closed religion that brooks no truths other than its own. Not even to condemn the Romans but political power that kills in the interest of maintaining peace and quiet" (p. 59).

We must always "handle with care" when it comes to how we "use" the Bible.

4)   Finally, in terms of negative clarifications, not only is the Bible not God, not one-dimensional, not to be used as a battering-ram; also, it is not the literal word of God. I do affirm that it certainly contains God's word, but some responsible sifting is necessary.

In his Beecher Lectures at Yale Divinity School in 1984 Krister Stendahl referred to 1 Corinthians 7:25: "Now concerning the unmarried, I have no command of the Lord, but I give my opinion as one who by the Lord's mercy is trustworthy." About this, Stendahl asks somewhat facetiously, "What do fundamentalists do when the Word of God says, 'This ain't the Word of God'?"

What I have hoped to illustrate in clarifying what the Bible is *not* is that the Bible is open to, requires, and is, in fact, the product of interpretation. We will return to this interpretive task as a part of saying in positive and even celebrative ways some of the things that the Bible *is*.

The Bible is a library of 66 books that over the decades and centuries the church came to agree upon as being expressive and revelatory of the energy or spirit of God at work in our world.

It is the record of humanity's growing understanding of God, not a static but a dynamic evolution revealing humanity's search for God and God's search for humanity.

The evolution of this library was a long process, taking perhaps a thousand years for the Hebrew scriptures to come into final formulation. This occurred in 90 A.D. at the Council of Jamnia. Representatives of the Jewish faith put their (or history's) stamp of approval on the 39 books that Christians came to call the Old Testament. We would do better simply to refer to these books as the Hebrew Scriptures.

Our New Testament also developed over an extended period of time, perhaps as much as 200 years. The 27 books that now make up the New Testament were written probably over a span of 75-80 years, and the New Testament was not authorized in its present form until 367 A.D.

At one time there were as many as 50 "gospels" in circulation in various parts of the early church (fragments or other references have been discovered), but only four made it into the final canon which early church leaders considered to be authoritative. As late as 150 A.D. a man named Marcion mounted an effort to limit the New Testament to the Gospel of Luke and the letters of Paul. Indeed, we can see that an evolutionary process was at work.

The Bible is a collection of different books and a variety of literary forms. It includes poetry, myths, legends, law, history, epistles (letters intended to be read to groups of people) and gospels (not what we think of as history, but more *celebrations of meaning*). The gospels reveal how the authors saw Jesus as God's "good news." The Bible even contains some tall tales with a moral lesson. It was first divided into chapters about 1250 A.D. and received its verse divisions in the Geneva Bible in 1560 A.D.

In *Rescuing the Bible from Fundamentalism,* Bishop Spong acknowledges that "the Bible is not literally true in a thousand details" (p.76). One need only compare the birth narratives in Matthew and Luke or the passion narratives in the four Gospels to see dramatic differences and discrepancies. But Spong stressed that the Bible does keep speaking of the deep wells of truth from which life springs, and so it continues to address our lives.

The Bible indeed deals with the timeless themes of bondage, exodus, deliverance, wilderness experiences, journeying toward a promised land, separation from God and from those we love, reconciliation, the struggle with death and the awesome gift of life in rich and full dimension.

It is because of the repetitive and effective surfacing of these great themes and deep wells of truth that the Bible can call us to a deeper understanding of what God is like and of what, by God's help, we may become. In fact, the whole purpose of Bible study is to discover more of what God is like and to continue asking how we can relate our conclusions to our own life experiences. Again, the interpretive process surfaces as essential in addressing and receiving the Biblical message.

Dr. Rick Lowery, Old Testament professor at Phillips Theological Seminary, tells a delightful illustrative story about the distinction between *truth* and *historical fact.*

It seems that a seminary professor in Africa was lecturing a class that was about evenly divided between urban and rural students. He told them about a donkey that was walking along when it came to a fork in the road. Down the right-hand fork he smelled food. Down the left-hand fork he smelled food. He started right, then left, then right, then left. He was so torn with indecision in his desire to proceed in both directions that he finally split in half and died.

"Now," asked the professor, "is that a *true* story?"

All of the urban students said it was not true. The rural students said it was true. They argued and argued. Eventually the rural students agreed with the urban students. No, they decided, it was not true. But there was one hold-out, one stubborn rural student who kept saying the story was true. Finally the professor, with a smile on his face, said to him, "Why is it true?"

"It is true," the student said, "because greed kills."

The Bible contains many kinds of literature, even some "tall tales" (as, for instance, in the first six chapters of the Book of Daniel– Daniel in the lion's den, the story of the fiery furnace and the handwriting on the wall) but they are "tall tales" *with significant points*. They are *true* in a very deep sense of that word.

So, the Bible is not God, not one-dimensional, not an excuse for self-righteousness and not the *literal* word of God. But it is a great and good book that calls us time and again to larger visions for living, reminding us that God is the source and resource for all of life. For Christians it points to Jesus as that one who shows us the way most fully into the heart of God, helping us under-stand what God would have us to be and to do. The Bible is true.

We should then treat the scriptures as Jesus treated them–with respect, but not with a defensive zeal for protecting them from study, examination and interpretation. The Bible is a window onto what God is like, not a hammer to judge and smash others, but a mirror in which to discover ourselves in encounter with God.

The Bible is a witness which testifies to the presence, power and purposes of the living God. It points the church to God; it is our most important source of the knowledge of God.

However, it is not our only source. We also use the tradition of the church outside the Bible from the second century to the present time; we use our awareness of our experience in the world; and we use human reason and the guiding of God's spirit in the interpretive process. Indeed, if God is present at all times and places, it is reasonable to assume that God can reveal God's self in a variety of ways. The Bible contains images and metaphors which alert us to this presence. Very simply, we read, study and interpret the Bible so that the spirit of God might emerge.

Once again, the key word is "interpretation." The Bible can be seen as a series of interpretations of God's presence in the world and through the arenas of human activity. Over many generations Biblical writers interpreted how God was present and active and, of course, used the language, thought forms and worldviews available to them in their culture.

Since the second century the interpretive process has continued. The Christological formulations of the fourth and fifth centuries are good illustrations, as faithful church leaders sought to understand, interpret and then express the meaning of Jesus Christ for their own age.

They understood the forces that moved in their world differently than we understand those forces today. For them a storm might be an immediate expression of the wrath of God (though that was not Jesus' understanding as seen in Matthew 5:43-48). However, for us a storm is the natural working out of certain weather patterns caused by winds, temperature variations and available moisture.

The world of the fourth and fifth centuries was inhabited by demons, unseen spirits who might do dastardly deeds or inhabit the bodies of otherwise normal people and cause them to run amok. Today we have a scientific perspective that tends to explain such phenomenon in terms of the effects of bad environment or abnormal brain chemistry.

Our interpretations today must, as much as possible, take seriously, though not finally, the cultural framework (language, thought forms, world-view) of the Biblical writers and the early church fathers as we seek to understand their words and motives. Only then can we take the further step of seeking application for us today in terms of our own culture and experiences.

Indeed, the interpretive process goes on and on. Certainly the world-view of our day is a far cry from that of the first century. As human beings we still have much in common with the people of all times, but there can be some significant differences in how we understand life.

Mark 9:14-29 offers an example of how position in time and one's world-view can affect how a story is received, as well as the validity and importance of some interpretation. This story clearly equates demon possession with epilepsy. That is a viewpoint few would share today. We understand that epilepsy reflects a problem with brain chemistry. Or what about the suggestion that deaf-muteness is the result of being invaded by an evil spirit? What person of compassion and a clear mind in today's world would burden a deaf or speechless child with the idea that the devil had possessed her or him.

So our scientific world-view alters how we hear the story, necessitating the articulation of certain clarifications. At the same time we can feel the "good news" emanating from this story as Mark celebrates Jesus as the one who overcomes evil in whatever guise it may appear. God's intention, as expressed in Jesus Christ, is for health and wholeness for his creation. And *that* is the truth.

31

Later, when we confront some of the Christological formulations, we will recognize that some of them adhere to an earlier world-view than may be meaningful for us today, especially in consideration of the diverse religious environment that will continue to become more complex in the 21st century.

Actually it is not so much the New Testament images (including Christ, Son of God, Son of man, good shepherd, way, truth, light of the world, and others) that create problems for the modern mind and for our cultural diversity. It is the images of the early church fathers and their propensity to claim for Jesus what he never seems to have claimed for himself, namely, being the same as God.

We will deal with these images in more detail in chapters 5-7.

Then there are the basic interpretive questions: who, what, when, where, why and how? So much in biblical interpretation depends, not just on our world-view, but on our personal point of view—that is, where we stand in relation to the story. For instance, who is doing the talking or writing, who is being addressed and what is the meat of the intended message?

Stendahl, again speaking at Yale Divinity School, warned against assuming that you already know the meaning of a much-told story. He illustrates with the story of the prodigal son as told in Luke 15. It is his contention that the story is told because there were some who did not like Jesus keeping company with *real* sinners. The addressee is the older brother, as well as all of those in our churches with an older brother mentality. Stendahl says that a sermon on this text should say something about the older brother being sort of "all right"–indispensable to the farm, dull but faithful. His only shortcoming (and for Jesus it is a big one) is his incapacity for rejoicing when his brother comes home. That, says Stendahl, is what the story is all about; that is the specificity of the setting to which the preacher (the interpreter) must try to be true.

I agree with Stendahl, but with the qualification that it is possible to change positions in the story. Are you "the older brother," "the prodigal son" or "the loving father" who loves both of his boys, but is overjoyed to see the "prodigal" come home? How the story is heard depends on your personal point of view.

A college student is reported to have recorded the following message on his answering machine: "Hi, this is Dave. If it's the phone company, I sent the money. If it's Mom or Dad, please send money. If it's financial aid, you didn't loan me enough money. If it's a coed, leave a message; I'll get back to you, and don't worry, I've got plenty of money." The message changes as the audience changes.

For instance, in terms of Christological formulations, we are not the same audience as that being addressed by Athanasius in the fourth century. For Athanasius the claiming of supernatural powers and identity with God for Jesus may have been important on several different fronts.

How could Jesus contend with demons who had supernatural powers unless he too possessed such powers? How could a mere mortal do combat with immortal beings? So, for Athanasius, given his world-view, Christ had to be presented as the "Godman."

There may also have been the political consideration that Athanasius' God (now the God of the Roman emperor as well) needed to be presented as more powerful than all the competing gods of other cultures and religions.

This would have had definite Christological ramifications. The risen Christ represented the unique feature of the Christian religion and the way to make Christ superior to all the competition was to make him co-equal with God.

Though these interpretations do not seem to carry the "sense of the scripture" or to evoke the humility of Philippians 2:5-9, they may have seemed necessary to the Roman Catholic bishops of 325 and 367 A.D.

They were not being hypocritical or fanciful. They were describing the meaning of the life and death of Jesus Christ in terms of how they understood the world in which they lived.

Of course, even those early church leaders were not of one mind, a bishop named Arius was declared a heretic for his strong insistence on emphasizing the humanity of Jesus.

And the outcome of the controversy was to settle on the "true God . . . and truly human" formula of Nicea (325 A.D.). This continues to raise very difficult questions because the world-view and political needs that shaped it were so different from our own.

Sometimes the problem is not that the message or world-view has changed, but that the interpreter has not understood the author's point of view. There can be loss of clarity over time as to the identity and purpose of the author.

When Knute Rockne first went to Notre Dame as football coach, the team had not done well the year before, and Rockne instituted a program of rigorous individual discipline and stringent team training. He set curfews and workout schedules, insisting on regular attendance and punctuality. When many of the veteran players continued to be late for practices and even missed some team meetings, scathing but anonymous editorials about the team and about individual players began to appear in the Southbend newspaper.

Team members did not like the negative press they were receiving and went to Rockne to complain. He was sympathetic and said he was offended by the editorials too. But he said he could not interfere with freedom of the press, and the only way to answer the charges of laziness and lack of discipline was for the players to shape up as individuals and as a team and not give that anonymous writer any more grist for his mill.

He told his players they could disprove what was being written by their discipline at practice and by their performance on the field. Well, with some anger and a lot of determination the team buckled down and won four of the last five games of the season–and then went on to have a great record under Rockne's coaching.

Of course, when that season was over, it was discovered that Rockne himself had been the author of the anonymous letters to the newspaper.

What if, a thousand years later, an archaeologist were to be excavating the rubble of the Southbend newspaper and find this series of articles berating the football team. He might logically conclude from the contents that the author of the letters disliked the football team and rejoiced in their mistakes. When, in fact, if the archaeologist knew the identity of the author and his relationship to the players, he would perceive the real intent of the letters. He would know Rockne's target was the team for whom he cared so deeply.

Once a woman dialed 911 because she was witnessing an emergency in her front yard. "We need help here right away!" The policeman on the other end said, "What's the problem, lady?" She responded, "That awful new postman is in the tree in my front yard teasing my pit bull." Surely the postman would have told the story differently.

This suggests the need for one more clarification about the interpretive process; that is, what is our "interpretive principle"?

We have recognized that the Bible is not one-dimensional, not a level playing field, so to speak. We value some passages more highly than others. On what basis can we make these decisions?

For instance, in 1 Samuel 15:1-3, the prophet Samuel tells Saul that God wants him to punish the Amalekites, to "kill both man and woman, infant and suckling, ox and sheep, camel and ass." Measure that against the spirit of God reflected in the 11th chapter of Hosea: "My heart recoils within me, my compassion grows warm and tender. I will not execute my fierce anger, I will not again destroy Ephraim; for I am God and not man, the Holy One in your midst, and I will not come to destroy."

Of course different people and different times are being addressed in these two passages, but in terms of what they reveal about what God is like, which do you vote for? And why?

Most of us will, I think, choose Hosea. Yes, the chauvinistic bias of Samuel in validating Israel's conquering of the land is bothersome. But the real clincher is that because of the gospel message of Jesus Christ, as well as other witnesses in the Hebrew Scriptures and the New Testament, we do not believe that God is in the business of killing little children or that God endorses such actions.

I believe that we interpret the Bible in the light of what Jesus said and how he lived to determine what God is like. Luther called Christ the "King of the Scriptures." By that he meant that all the contents of the Bible are to be evaluated on the basis of how they testify to God's grace. That, for most of us, is our "interpretive principle."

This is akin to Michael Kinnamon's understanding of how the scripture is authoritative. The *Word* (God's grace) stands in judgment of *the words* of the text. Another way of expressing it is that our growing understanding of what Christ's spirit requires provides the *spectacles* through which we interpret the words of scripture.

We shall soon see how that is applied to the various Christological metaphors. But first, one more essential in our stage-setting: how we nuance our language in talking about God.

Let us underscore with Dr. Fred Craddock, and many other Christian scholars, the affirmation that Christology should serve theology. The fundamental belief of the church, that there is one God, is the same as the fundamental belief of the synagogue. Whatever views we have of Christ or of the Holy Spirit must grow out of our understanding of God. It is regrettable that many Christians seem to accept the equation that the Jews believe in God and that we believe in Christ. That is a basically un-christian dichotomy. Jesus always pointed beyond himself to God as source and resource for living.

So, what can we say about what God is like in words that carry meaning for our own time?

❂ What About the Bible? ❂
Chapter Two Questions for Study and Discussion

1. Some people choose not to think about things they don't think about. The critical question is do we *think* about things we do think about?
   Can you give some examples of the Bible:
   >   1) contradicting itself?
   >   2) interpreting itself?
   >   3) presenting different points of view on the same issue?
   Do these threaten your belief in God?

2. Is there a difference in the moral perspective in Ezekiel 18 compared with Exodus 20:5?

3. How does the idea of "Jesus' return" affect your daily living? Which approach do you prefer: Mark 9:1, 2 Peter 3:8-9 or John 5:24?

4. What is the purpose of Bible study?

5. Is there a difference between "true" and "factual"?

6. Can our world-view affect the way we read the Bible? What about "point of view"?

7. Which is a better reflection of what God is like: 1 Samuel 15:1-3 or Hosea 11:8-9?

8. What is your "interpretive principle"?

3

Nuancing Our Language About God

This book is written in the sure and certain knowledge that terrible, evil things can and do happen. The effects of unleashed evil can be seen in the skeletal remains of war-bombed buildings, families bereft because of the violent death of loved ones, and our own vulnerability to random, mindless acts of terror. All of these became shockingly more real for me and thousands of others in the bombing of the Murrah Federal Building at 9:02 a.m. on April 19, 1995, in Oklahoma City, where I have lived for most of my life, and where I have ministered for the past 29 years.

Our city, the nation and the world were stunned by the horror of the blast and the death and destruction that resulted. First Christian Church, which I pastor, became the Family Disaster/Relief Center for families who had loved ones missing in the bombing. Also, it served as headquarters for the Red Cross and other relief agencies.

Counseling teams were set up, composed of clergy, mental health professionals and representatives of the funeral industry. For three weeks families continued to come to the church for nurture, support and information, desperately hoping that their loved ones would be found alive.

It turned out that after the first 24 hours all news was bad. But the city's heroes, the firemen, construction workers and rescue teams, continued their awesome task of braving the environs of a devastated building, hoping to find survivors and facing the horror of bringing out the bodies of the dead. Counselors were made available to respond to the emotional needs of these rescue workers as well.

The media were ever-present and, for the most part, demonstrated compassion and sensitivity to the victims' families and survivors. Interviews were conducted by worldwide media almost around the clock as a stunned public sought to make some sense of an absolutely senseless act. Words multiplied on words.

I personally gave dozens of responses to television, radio and print reporters, feeling that the clergy had a special responsibility to try to speak words of comfort and interpretation about such a devastating event. One of the first questions asked was, "Where was God in all of this?"

Again and again I said that I believed God's heart was the first to break when that bomb exploded, that God had been shut out of the hearts of the perpetrators, or they would not have committed this atrocity. God's "intentional" will for creation was not served by this insanity. In fact, it was, in that moment, defeated. Leslie Weatherhead's book, *The Will of God,* written in response to the horrors of World War II, offers helpful insight into such questions.

Indeed, evil erupted and interrupted God's creative activity. Immediately the issue becomes not one of "why did this happen?" It was evil and should not have occurred–no rationalizations can make it all right. The issue becomes "how can we respond and help?"

The response of the local community, the nation and the world (for instance, flowers for all the families sent anonymously from Belgium the day after the blast) said loudly and clearly that we were not going to let a moment of insanity define our humanity. Consequently, the human response became revelatory of God's will and activity in the world and elevated our sense of what it means to be human.

Times of crisis often provide very teachable moments that can be valuable theological experiences as well. Everything said at such times is magnified in significance. Spoken words are bound to communicate to others our deepest sense of what we think God is like. If we speak shallow words, if we are glib and too quick in our response, we may trivialize the image of the God whom we seek to serve.

We must, therefore, take care that there is heart in our words, because there is indeed heart in our God. We must take care not to speak formulas not rigorously examined about God that may have served another age or culture but are no longer adequate or appropriate to our own.

There are some things in such a teachable, theological moment that ought not to be said–and yet, I heard them said in the aftermath of the bombing. They were said with sincerity and with some conviction (though surely for the most part unquestioned), and often the speaker seemed unaware of the implications of his or her words.

I give here several examples because they illustrate how important it is to continually consider the ramifications of what we say, to understand the nuances of our language and especially of our language about God.

A woman from a town in southwestern Oklahoma called to express her care and concern, and then in a kind of awkward frustration she said, "Well, we just have to know that somehow everything fits in God's plan."

Oh, I hope not! I hope that the horrors of the Crusades and the Inquisition and the Salem witch trials and the Holocaust and the

April 19th explosion in Oklahoma City are seen and proclaimed as terrible denials of what God wants for humanity—definitely not a part of God's plan.

The Calvinistic legacy (whether it is what John Calvin intended or not) of a simplistic predestinarianism may have spoken to some people in a former age but certainly does not speak to many in ours. Furthermore, such a stance is not necessary as a protection for God's omnipotence—as we shall see when we affirm God as *creator* later in this chapter.

Further, I don't believe that Paul would want the passage in Romans 8:28 to be pressed into service at this juncture. It is one thing to say "that in everything God works for good with those who love him," and quite another to say that everything that happens is good. The bombing of the Murrah Federal Building was not good, though much goodness emerged in response to it.

Then there was the man who exited from church on the Sunday after the blast expressing how deeply grateful he and his wife were that their son, who worked in the Murrah Building, had escaped injury. He rejoiced with the words, "We got our miracle!" Now if you use the word "miracle" to describe "an unusually marvelous event," then, yes, that was a miracle. But, if you use the word as it is popularly understood as a "supernatural act," "a divine act," "God's intervention," then God acted capriciously—saving some while letting others die.

Surely we worship a God who is neither cruel nor capricious. We cannot say all that God *is*, but we can, being created in the image of God and with the gospel as our guide, say some things that God is *not*. God is not cruel; God is not capricious. There were no *choices* made by God in this event. The explosion was an act of evil. For some people to survive, while innocent children and others were killed, is not an expression of what God is like.

My theological/philosophical affirmation is that God is always more than the best that we can humanly conceive, never less than the best we can humanly conceive.

Rabbi Daniel Shevitz of Emanuel Synagogue in Oklahoma City told of letters he received from friends in Israel who were survivors of the Holocaust. He thought they might say, "Now you understand," but instead their message was, "Now you don't understand either."

If we could truly understand how such a thing could happen, it would in some sense diminish our humanity.

We can only say it happened because there is ignorance and warped thinking and evil in the world. Evil thoughts and evil actions bear evil consequences.

Such an event forces us to re-examine and reformulate what has sometimes become slipshod or at least outmoded theological perspective.

The crucifixion, for instance, was evil. Could great good, even a powerful new religious thrust, be wrought from it? Yes! But in and of itself it was evil. God did not want it. The same is true concerning the awful bombing on April 19, 1995, that took 168 lives and left hundreds physically and emotionally scarred.

I heard another man say, in an effort to encourage several families, "If God is good, your loved ones will be found alive." The man who spoke those words meant well; I know he did. But we must examine our words and take care how we speak, because that would say to some, when so many are found *not alive*, "Then God is not good." The words were wrong because they said the wrong thing about God.

There is a poem by Edgar A. Guest entitled "To All Parents" that was often quoted in the weeks immediately following the blast. In the midst of grief and loss sometimes words that simply drip with sentiment can seem to comfort, but I believe they are short-term comforts if they say the wrong thing about what God is like.

The poem says, *It may be six or seven years or twenty-two or three, but will you, 'til I call him back, take care of him for me*— suggesting that God is the active instrument of taking our children away from us. A later verse carries the same import, *Will you give him all your love, nor think the labor vain, nor hate me when I come to call to take him back again?*

God does not manipulate or directly control human events. Are we just puppets on the end of some cosmic strings, OR is there real significance in our decisions and choices? There is real significance *only* if God has released us in the process of creation into real freedom where we make real choices and real decisions; our "yes" means "yes," our "no" means "no," our prejudices can hurt others, and our loving kindness matters.

Again, **God does not manipulate or directly control human events**. Statements such as this are what I have in mind when I talk about "nuancing our language about God." So it becomes an inappropriate question to ask, "How could God allow this to happen?" Because this approach assumes that God could have stopped it from happening.

In the common sense vernacular, I am with Rabbi Harold Kushner, author of *When Bad Things Happen to Good People*, in preferring to give up some of God's power to hold on to God's love. But in a larger sense God's omnipotence should not be understood as the power to manipulate our daily lives, but as the power or energy that stands behind and makes all being possible.

How we respond to that power is our responsibility. That is the real freedom that gives real meaning to our lives.

Everything we say about God is, of course, metaphorical. We need to be very clear about that. Otherwise, we would be claiming that our words were God, and that would be idolatrous. So we look for metaphors that can be most helpful in conveying what we believe God is like.

I see God in images of loving kindness, in images that call light out of darkness, order out of chaos, in images that suggest liberation and responsibility–not in images that are devious, cruel or capricious.

Of course, the question must be faced. If God does not manipulate or control human events, how is God present in our world? How is God more than just a clock-maker who put it all together, wound it up and let it go?

I would affirm that *God's energy* is powerfully at work in our world and in us and through us to accomplish God's purposes. Let us call this "suasion."

It is the push of God's will for goodness to emerge from even the most heinous and evil of situations. It is light overcoming the darkness. It is Jesus on the cross saying, "Father, forgive . . ."

After the Murrah Building bombing, the people of Oklahoma did not allow that moment of insanity to define their humanity. Neither do we allow a moment of insanity to tell us what God is like.

I turn now to three of the images (ways of talking about God) that have been most consistently used in the tradition of the church and in theological discussion: Creator, Judge and Redeemer.

The Christian faith begins with God. I believe that is foundational. But how do we describe God? What are some of the *dimensions* of God's being?

45

When we think of God as "Creator," we want to have in mind more than magic poofs of smoke in a six-day whirlwind of activity. As an analogy I like to think of the marvelous mix of forces that causes new human life to come into being–the urge and joy of sexual union, the long months of quiet, turbulent, mysterious growth in the mother's womb, the intense pain of the birthing process, the burst of breath, the beauty of the first cries of the newborn, the relief and joy of the family in the focusing of potential for life in this little baby.

Samuel Miller summed it up beautifully in his book, *The Dilemma of Modern Belief*–"No poem is written, no picture painted, no music made, no sinner forgiven, no child born, no man loved, no truth known . . . except grace took a risk, bore a burden, absorbed the evil and suffered the pain." (p. 57-58) What a marvelous description of what "creation" is about–God, in love, taking risk–not a sure thing, but full of hope and potential and splendor.

Part of that *risk* is seen in the affirmation in Genesis 1:26 that we are created "in the image and likeness of God" and given "dominion." In creation God shares his creative and ordering energy. That is risky. You see, we are not only asking what do we believe God is like, but we are also asking what do we believe we should become. If God is creator, then we are to be creative. The affirmation is both theological and anthropological. We say something about the nature of the created when we describe the creator. An anonymous verse phrased it this way:

> *Isn't it strange that princes and kings*
> *And clowns that caper in sawdust rings*
> *And common people like you and me*
> *Are builders with God in eternity?*
> *Each is given a book of rules,*
> *A shapeless mass and a set of tools,*
> *And each must build, ere life has flown,*
> *A stumbling block or a stepping stone.*

We are not only called into being but into responsible being. To refer to God as creator is to say something definitive about human origins and about human direction and loyalty.

Another dimension about God as creator is to affirm creation as an ongoing process rather than a finished product. This is suggested by the alternate translation of Genesis 1:1 as footnoted in the Revised Standard Version, "In the beginning *when God began to create* the heavens and the earth . . ." Dr. Rick Lowery, Old Testament Professor at Phillips Theological Seminary, sees this as the more appropriate rendering of the Hebrew. Thus, the act of creation is still going on and has to do with ordering the *tohu va bohu*, the chaos, the desert waste, the disordered mess.

This suggests that God is not the matter out of which life is formed, but God becomes "the heart of the matter." This will be seen to have Christological implications. What was "the intentionality of God" when God began to create, and how does that find expression in Jesus Christ?

To speak of God as "Judge" is to stir images of a fierce, angry, even vindictive jurist almost eager to slam the gates of hell against those who cross him. Actually this is more of an American revivalist notion than the dominant picture in the Hebrew Scriptures. Jonathan Edwards certainly gave expression to it in his sermon, "Sinners in the Hands of an Angry God." Still this is not what the best in the Judaeo-Christian tradition has meant to emphasize when referring to God as judge.

What we have meant in the tradition of the church is to underscore that there is moral dimension in the being of God. That is, God cares about responsibility and accountability. There are more and less appropriate ways of relating to one another and the world in which we live. There are demands of justice from which even love (or especially love) is not exempt. God cares about how we treat our fellow human beings. That God's love is unconditional

47

does not mean that it is undemanding.

William Muehl in his 1985 Beecher Lectures at Yale Divinity School and in his subsequent book, *Why Preach? Why Listen?,* describes a counseling session he conducted for a couple he had married several years before. At one point in the conversation the husband had just finished some blatantly self-serving statement when the wife interrupted, saying how unfair he was. The husband at this juncture looked at his wife with a hooded glance and said throatily, "When we were married, I promised to love you, not be fair to you."

At this romantic gambit the foolish young woman threw herself into her husband's arms and they were reconciled just long enough to conceive a child. Then the marriage ended in divorce, and two years later Bob, the husband, killed himself.

Muehl says, "Bob was not destroyed by some thunderbolt from heaven . . . Bob destroyed himself by ignoring the structures of justice from which even love is not exempt" (p. 62-63). The point is clear: love without ingredients of judgment, responsibility and simple fairness dehumanizes and is not loving.

In nuancing our language about God we are saying that as human beings created by God we are to be responsible and, yes, held accountable for how we treat one another. The Ten Commandments and the Golden Rule are based on that assumption.

A three-year-old boy's parents found him crying uncontrollably at the kitchen table. He had a pile of pennies in front of him and had swallowed one. He was convinced he was going to die. No amount of talking could change his mind.

Desperate to calm him his father palmed one of the pennies and pretended to pull it from the little boy's ear. The boy was immediately relieved and delighted. In a flash he snatched the penny from his father's hand, popped it into his mouth and swallowed it. He then demanded cheerfully, "Do it again, Dad!"

Often we are like that little boy, infantile in our approach to life, wanting Dad or God to keep making things right when much of that power (accountability and responsibility) already resides with us. We need to rekindle that dimension of our understanding of what God is like and wants us to become.

Further, in the Christian tradition, we have also consistently understood God as "Redeemer"–one who keeps drawing us back onto the right road, one who yearns for his creation to reclaim those characteristics which make for right relationships, for health and wholeness in living. Forgiveness and reclamation are central chambers in the heart of God.

For Christians, Jesus is the most specific way in which we see the redemptive activity of God being expressed. As the hymn says, *O Jesus, blest redeemer, sent from the heart of God, hold us who wait before thee, near to the heart of God.*

It is under the heading of God as redeemer that Jesus of Nazareth comes to center stage. For Christians, Jesus is a primary lens, though not the only lens, through which we see God's redemptive activity.

The human problem is separation, whether the result of sin or slavery or exile. In *Meeting Jesus Again For the First Time,* Marcus Borg shows how the great stories of the Bible specify each of these conditions–sin, slavery, exile–as occasions for God's redemption activity.

God's work isn't just creation but restoration, not just the gift of life in the first place but the chance to claim it new and fresh even after we have messed it up. How gracious and loving God is!!!

However, redemption is not a "green stamp" transaction, trading Jesus' life for our sins. Jesus did not come to die, contrary to much revivalist preaching even in our own day.

Jesus did not come to die but to teach us how to live. But his dying, sometimes especially his dying, can be part of that lesson.

There is, as Dietrich Bonhoeffer expressed so vividly with his own words and actions, a cost to discipleship.

Too often in today's world the affirmation of God's grace has become equated with making life *easy*. What God's redemptive grace does, as seen in Jesus Christ and other channels as well, is to make life possible again and again and again, but not easy.

God's grace does not cancel the need for effort, commitment, love and hard work; it sets a context in which these realities make sense. God's redemptive grace authorizes effort, commitment, love and hard work and gives us more than one chance at life.

Jesus did not come to make life easy but to give us the chance to really live. The gift of Jesus is to show us the terms on which life is possible, how life can be lived significantly.

We will explore further the ramifications of God's redemptive grace for our Christological understanding in later chapters. Suffice it here to say that we do affirm an intimacy of relationship between God and Jesus without having to say that, therefore, Jesus is God.

There is one more approach to the nuancing of our language about God that has proved helpful to me. The question here is not the question of the existence of God as an ontological (branch of metaphysics dealing with the nature of being) concern, but more the question of the importance of God, a functional concern. That is, how is God present in our world, and how does God make a difference for us?

For example, to believe that God exists the way you believe the South Pole exists, simply as an abstract point of reference that makes no difference in the conduct of daily life, is not a religious stance. The issue is not "Does God exist?" The issue is "What kind of people do we become when we attach ourselves to God? What meaning does God have for us?" That is our quest.

One answer to that can be framed in terms of what Rabbi Harold Schulweis of Los Angeles, California, has referred to as "Predicate Theology." In English grammar we learn that when the verb in a sentence is a form of the infinitive "to be" (am, are, is, was, have been, etc.), the part that comes after the verb is not called an object (since the verb "to be" is a linking verb and does not denote action) but is known as the predicate.

"Predicate Theology" means that when we find statements about God, such as "God is love," "God is truth," "God is a friend of the poor," we concentrate on the predicate rather than the subject. Those are not just statements about God, but they tell us that loving, being true and befriending the poor are divine activities. When these things happen, God is present.

The appropriate theological question, then, becomes not "Where is God?" but "When is God?" Being in God's presence or "near to the heart of God" becomes a matter, not of being in the right place, but of doing the right things or being the right kind of person in given situations.

One day Mark Twain was walking down the street, when, on the other side of the street, he saw a man beating a dog. He rushed across the street, grabbed the man's arm and said, "Quit beating that dog." The man responded, "You mind your own business. This is my dog and I'll beat him if I want to." Whereupon Twain is reported to have responded, "This is my business because that

51

is God's dog and God sent me here to protect him." That is a good example of Predicate Theology.

Psalm 146:8-9 says, *The Lord sets the prisoners free; the Lord opens the eyes of the blind. The Lord lifts up those who are bowed down; the Lord loves the righteous. The Lord watches over the sojourners, he upholds the widow and the fatherless; but the way of the wicked he brings to ruin.* That is Predicate Theology.

In this kind of thinking an atheist is not a person who says, "God has no meaning for me," but one who says, "Helping the poor and hungry, working for justice and loving my family have no meaning for me."

When is God? When you care, when you reach out and touch the lonely, when you are patient and kind in circumstances that would seem to dictate otherwise, when you are not exclusive, but inclusive, in your love for the world, when you fight for the quality of another's life–whether a dog, a child or a senior citizen. When is God? Every time someone cares and does something about it, that is when God happens.

So in various ways we can nuance our language about God, knowing that we speak metaphorically, knowing that we cannot say everything that God is, but that we can with some firmness, resolve and clarity say some of the things God is not.

My philosophical guideline says that God is always more than the best that we can conceive, but because we are made in God's image and likeness and have the gospel of God's grace in Jesus Christ as a reference point and interpretive principle, God is never less than the best we can conceive.

God is the sacred at the center of our existence, the holy mystery that surrounds us and is within us. God is the One, as Paul says, "in whom we live and move and have our being" (Acts 17:28).

I believe in God–not just as a theological concept, but more importantly, as a caring and sustaining presence.

➤ ➤ ⬅ ⬅

◈ Nuancing Our Language About God ◈
Chapter Three Questions for Study and Discussion

1. Does God directly intervene in human affairs? Is God capricious? Is God cruel?

2. How would phrases like "God's plan" and "We got our miracle" affect your thinking about God if your loved one was killed when others survived?

3. What images or metaphors are most descriptive of what God is like?

4. What does the phrase "builders with God" suggest about human responsibilities and the "intentionality of God" where human life is concerned?

5. What does "love" look like? Can it be defined without reference to justice? Does "unconditional love" mean "no demands," "no expectations"?

6. Did God plan Jesus' death?

7. When is God?

4

Does God Play Favorites?
Thoughts about Prayer

Does God play favorites? Surely, we know, God wants what is best, wholeness and health, for all his creation. But, except in that very broad and general sense, we have to say that, in particulars, God does not play favorites.

Jesus says in Matthew 5 that God sends his rain on the just and the unjust and makes his sun to shine on the good and the bad alike. In that sense, you see, God's blessings are indiscriminate. God does not play favorites.

In Luke 13 you will remember there was the dialogue between Jesus and the disciples about the tower at Siloam that had fallen. The disciples were asking Jesus if the 18 who had been killed were especially bad sinners, worse than the other Galileans, and was that why they had died? Jesus answered clearly, no, that was not the case. Accidents, you see, do happen. God does not play favorites.

Yet, some would ask, if God does not play favorites, why pray?

When first presenting some of these materials to a district ministers' gathering, I made the statement from the chapter on "Nuancing Our Language About God" that *God does not manipulate or directly control human events.*

One of the ministers, tongue-in-cheek, smile on face, twinkle in the eye, interrupted with the question, "Then why pray?"

He didn't really believe that the purpose of prayer is to get God to change the circumstances of our lives in order to make us happier or wealthier. But he was reflecting a common misconception that often seems to pervade the popular understanding of prayer.

The purpose of prayer is not to get God to *tune in* to us but to get us *in tune* with God. Prayer at its best is not about getting a living but about getting a life, not just having enough to live on but having enough to live for, about getting more *in touch* with God.

Norman Pittenger has said that in prayer it is not that we persuade God to do what God has hitherto been unwilling to do. It is not that we inform God of what previously God had not known. It is not that we engage in an arm-twisting of deity. Rather it is that we "attend" to God. By means of such attention we become responsive to the God whose loving activity and hence loving presence, is always with us.

Dr. Fred Craddock, in his introductory course on preaching at Candler School of Theology, would share 18 statements about preaching with his new students. The last on that list says, "Build an altar in every sermon, because praying and preaching are twins. It is speaking *with* God which gives authority to speaking *about* God."

In the preceding chapter I talked a lot *about God*. I hope that what was said will gain further *authorization* as we explore the awesome privilege of speaking *with God*.

I want to talk about prayer in terms of *expectation* and *cultivation*.

Over the years several real-life conversations have continued to re-focus my concern about the need for a better understanding of prayer.

Once at a church group men's dinner I overheard two young men complaining about the pace of their personal and professional lives. One said, "I'm so busy I never catch up with myself." The second said quite simply, "My life is out of control."

Not long ago at a meeting of our church staff, our Director of Children's Education was bemoaning much the same sense of perplexity. She said, "There isn't enough time. I was in the car yesterday from 5:15 to 7:15 just getting the boys to their different events, then did my grocery shopping and didn't get home until 8:30. How can we hold it all together?"

A few days after the Murrah Building bombing in 1995, a young woman volunteer, overwhelmed by the awfulness of the tragedy and the grief of the victims' families, asked in real emotional distress, "How can we know God is still there? How can we feel God more personally?"

And finally, a young couple who had been visiting our church for some time told me of their confusion and concern over a tragedy in their lives. Several years before, her father had died. Her husband had grown very close to his father-in-law, had found in him a friend and confidant. Her husband in anguish said, "I loved my father-in-law. He was too young to die. I prayed hard and long *in Jesus' name,* but still he died."

There is an oft-quoted story about a preacher who was anxiously trying to prepare his Sunday sermon while his eight-year-old son ran noisily in and out of the room.

In a creative effort to corral the little boy's energies he gave him a newspaper picture of a map of the world, all torn into little pieces, and challenged him to put the world back together. The father thought it would gain him at least an hour of uninterrupted study time. After all, the little boy knew nothing about world geography.

But, in ten minutes the boy was back with the puzzle solved. "How did you do it so quickly?" his father asked.

"Oh, it was easy," said the boy, "There was a picture of a man on the back and I found if I got the man right, the world would be right."

Jesus made it clear that prayer is central to the life of faith, and if we can get our prayer life right, then the rest of life will be better.

Sometimes we are disappointed in prayer (and in God) because our expectations are wrong, sincere but sincerely mistaken. An overly simplistic, petition-oriented approach to prayer has set us up for disappointment and disillusionment.

At times this misunderstanding of the purpose of prayer has been fostered by certain televangelists or self-appointed, religious gurus who use petition (asking) prayers of healing for commercial leverage with their followers.

There are even specific scriptures which, when taken literally, encourage the idea that prayer is simply the means of gaining God's attention for our shopping list.

Texts such as Matthew 17:21 ("if you have faith as a grain of mustard seed . . . nothing will be impossible to you.") and John 14:13-14 ("Whatever you ask in my name, I will do it . . . if you ask anything in my name, I will do it.") should be taken seriously, but not literally.

We've already referred to the "figure of speech" usage by Jesus of faith that can move mountains–a way of saying faith can do great things.

Now we need to bring some interpretive perspective to the text in John 14 because a literalistic emphasis has caused otherwise responsible, thoughtful people to think of God as a great vending machine in the sky, doling out answers to requests that come accompanied by the coin of Jesus' name.

We must ask, what did Jesus mean or what did John mean by putting these words in Jesus' mouth? It should be noted that this statement by Jesus appears in none of the other gospels.

Option number one: Leslie Weatherhead suggested many years ago that in the ancient Near East *name* was always identified with *purpose*. One possibility is that Jesus was saying, "Anything you ask that is in accord with my purposes, I will do it."

But even that may encourage an overly literal expectation of quid pro quo results. Surely the health of loved ones is in accord with God's purposes as seen in Jesus Christ. The son-in-law who prayed that his wife's father wouldn't die (and he had prayed in Jesus' name) was understandably disappointed, and his faith was shaken when his father-in-law died anyway.

The point to be made here is that health and wholeness for all creation is in accord with God's purposes, *but not in a simplistic way.*

God does not manipulate or directly control human events. To do so would turn the natural order upside down, the relatively dependable order of natural law into a shambles.

What kind of a world would it be if gravity only worked some of the time? What if my prayers "in Jesus' name" could get me a promotion even when I did not earn it? And what if my exercise of free will never damaged my neighbor because I prayed for God to put things back in order when I was at fault? Like the little boy who had swallowed the penny, and then on being rescued by an imaginative father, immediately swallowed another penny saying, "Hey, Dad, do it again!"

Paul said in 1 Corinthians 13 that when he was a child he thought as a child, but that when he grew up, he gave up childish ways.

We must see that sometimes our choices or the nature of the world we live in can set into motion a chain reaction of cause and effect that God must not interrupt. For if God were to directly intervene, then either this world would not be a dependable world to live in or God would be seen as arbitrary, capricious and manipulative; and those are not the characteristics of the God revealed in the best of the Biblical revelation.

Option number two: Another way of looking at the John 14 text is to reinterpret the words, asking, "What was Jesus getting at? What did he mean to convey to the disciples?"

Perhaps what Jesus was saying was, "Men, I love you, I'll do anything in the world *I can* for you." Much as any of us may have expressed a similar emotion to our children or a really good friend, Jesus is saying, "If it is in my power, I will do it."

The operative words *I can* are immensely important. There are some things *given the nature of reality* that we cannot do, and there are some things Jesus could not do. Remember his prayer in the Garden of Gethsemane, "Father, if possible, let this cup pass. . . ." It may not be possible that certain goals could be achieved unless the cup stays right where it is. Jesus' words should be read as a statement of devotion to his followers, not an invitation to a shopping spree.

There are other subtle situations where the gospel record indicates that Jesus would not interrupt the flow of the natural order.

He would not manipulate the weather. He affirmed in Matthew 5 that God sends his rain on the just and unjust alike. (Though Jesus was the one in another setting who calmed the storms of life, we take that figuratively or metaphorically.)

He resisted the temptation to define his ministry by magic. He would not turn stones into bread and he would not jump off the Temple just to impress the crowds.

So, again, why pray? We do not pray to get God on our side. God is already on our side in all the ways that really count. God is with us and wants the best for us.

That is what William Sloan Coffin, Jr. meant when, after his 24 year-old son was killed in an auto accident, he said, "God's heart was the first to break when my son's car went through the guard rail into the bay."

In summary we pray, I believe, for several very positive reasons.

1)   We pray to practice and affirm the nearness of God. C. H. Dodd has said that prayer is the divine in us appealing to the divine above us.

We pray to be in touch with God.

2)   We pray seeking intunement with God. The point is not to get God tuned to us but to get us tuned in to God. Coffin says that prayer is seeing through God's eyes. We pray to see life and people and things as God sees them. We pray to know the will of God.

We pray to be in tune with God.

3)   We pray as a means of focusing our own internal (but God-given) resources so that, whatever bumps and bruises life brings, we will be better able to respond. Our prayers don't change God; they change us. Prayer doesn't always make things better, but

prayer can make us better for whatever may come against us. *We pray to be internally and spiritually more able*.

Prayer isn't magical incantation. It does not bring rain to parched soil, but it can bring relief to a weary soul.

If we turn to prayer with the right expectations, prayer will not disappoint us. It is the reminder and reassurance that God is, that God cares and that God is *with us* in any and all circumstances. God hurts with our hurts and rejoices with our joys.

In Luke 11 the disciples ask Jesus to teach them how to pray, and he responds with what we now call "The Lord's Prayer."

Two interpretive comments: First, *prayer is not simple*. Otherwise the disciples would not have had to make this request. If prayer were simple, something that just anybody could do, something totally on the surface, then why the request, "Lord, teach us to pray"?

We have suggested for too long that prayer was just saying what was in our hearts. It is that, and I believe that prayer is available to everyone of us, but I also believe that there are those who do it better than others, those from whom we can learn.

We can learn to pray better and doing so is a lifelong journey. As wonderful as they were, the prayers we learned as children are not adequate to adult dilemmas.

Do say what is on your heart, but then understand that prayer is learning and listening. It requires patience and courage. As we pray we should be asking, "Is this what I should pray for?"

Our prayer life will get better as we know God better, and we will know God better as we work at our prayer life. We must be persistent and consistent if we would learn to pray.

Secondly, *there are no singular personal pronouns in "The Lord's Prayer" except the one that refers to God.* All of the other pronouns in "The Lord's Prayer" are plural.

What is the manner of the prayer that Jesus teaches? His approach suggests that prayer is communal. We do pray for self, but in the context of community. To pray as Jesus taught means to pray *for* others and to pray *with* others.

Two Jewish men were on the way to synagogue and were greeted by a third. The third man asked, "Benjamin, why are you going to synagogue? You don't even believe in God." Benjamin responded, "My friend Harry is going to synagogue to talk to God. I am going to synagogue to talk to my friend Harry."

That is not bad, you know, because while he is there talking to Harry, he is going to be part of a praying community, and it just may be that a little bit of him will also be talking to God.

We need one another. We need the community of faith. We need books of great devotion. We need to study what others have said and done about prayer.

There are, of course, different kinds of prayer–prayers of adoration, confession, thanksgiving and supplication (or petition). It makes a nice acronym–ACTS.

We can see how prayers of adoration, confession and thanksgiving put us *in touch* and *in tune* with God. It is the prayers of supplication or petition that give us trouble.

When we ask if God hears our prayers, we are not asking if God hears our praise (adoration) or confession or thanksgiving. What we really wonder about is whether and how God hears our requests.

So, what kinds of prayers of petition and supplication are appropriate in this learning process of prayer?

A man was given a tour of the heavenly post office where the responses to prayers were sent out. He walked into the mail room, and it looked to him as if all of the packages were simply packets of seeds. And he said to the heavenly postmaster, "What's this?" "Well," said the postmaster, "take a look."

So he picked up a package and it said, "seed of courage" and he picked up another and it said, "seed of patience" and another "seed of cheerfulness."

"These are wonderful," he said. "It seems to me these are just what people would want."

The postmaster said, "No, no. It is what they *need*, but not what they *want*. What they *want* is for us to send them the flowers, but what they need is the seed. Because, you know, the flowers are not easy to send. Once they're cut they wilt and wither. But the seed, when planted in good soil, puts down deep roots and brings back crop after crop."

Whether prayers center on adoration, confession, thanksgiving or supplication, may we learn to pray for needs instead of wants, to be more grown up in our expectation and cultivation of prayer.

What about the *cultivation* of prayer? Our prayer life will be better if we keep turning the soil. Sometimes we may *think* our way into new modes of acting, but more of the time, we will *act* our way into new levels of thinking. Prayer needs practice. We get better at it by doing it.

A little boy was flying his kite on a cloudy day. He stood there holding this stick with string wrapped around it, but the kite was hidden in the clouds. "What are you doing?" asked a man walking by. "Oh," answered the boy, "I'm flying my kite." "But," replied the man, "how do you know it's there, you can't see it." "That's easy," the boy responded, "I can feel the tug on the string."

I truly believe that the more we practice prayer, the more we will feel the tug on our heart. It is the wind of God's spirit. Perhaps that is what Paul is suggesting when he says in 1 Thessalonians 5:17: "Rejoice always, pray constantly, give thanks in all circumstances; for this is the will of God in Christ Jesus for you." Yes, practice, practice, practice!

Human beings can be the language of God. In 1992 following a heart attack and bypass surgery, I was more conscious of prayer, my own and the prayers of others for me. During my recuperation I was helped to feel the caring of God through the caring of others. I felt strongly God's sustaining presence, the tug on the string.

The Bible and other great literature can also be the language of God. We read the story of the Good Samaritan or the Prodigal Son and we feel the tug of God's presence on our lives. Reading good devotional materials can be part of "praying constantly," part of the cultivation of the sense of God, part of planting the right seed.

This cultivation of the sense of God has to do with time, with listening, with thinking and doing.

If life seems out of control, if we are having a difficult time holding it all together, if we want to feel God more personally, then perhaps we should pray about it. That is, take time to meditate, to think, to reconsider our priorities, to evaluate the options, to consult with God.

We may not get *magical* results, but I do believe we will get *meaningful* results. If we take the time to listen, think and do, we will feel the tug of God's presence on our lives. We will know God is there, and we will grow to know God better.

It is important not to expect a quick fix. For prayer to bring "the peace that passes understanding" requires practice, cultivation, water, sunlight and time for the seed to grow.

Alexander Campbell used to talk about "coming within an understanding distance of God." Dr. Fred Craddock enlarged on that theme in *Overhearing the Gospel* when he said, "Lifetime questions take a lifetime; questions of conscience require conscience; issues of morals and religion can be handled only after one has achieved some size, some dimensions of pathos, sympathy, concern and sensitivity. There is an understanding peculiar to the righteous person, to the person who lives within an understanding distance of God" (p. 36).

Many years ago (more than I choose to enumerate in public) we had a cook at our fraternity house at the University of Oklahoma whose nickname was appropriately "Cookie." She was always patient and gracious with the sophomoric prattling and teasing of all the guys. The only time she ever seemed in a hurry was at Sunday morning breakfast. She would cook eggs "to order" but only until 10 a.m., when she would hurry out the door to go to church.

One Sunday, a number of us were standing around as "Cookie" made ready to leave and one of the boys said, "Cookie, do you always go to church? Doesn't it get a little boring?"

Cookie's response stayed with us all and has continued to stretch my sense of things spiritual. She said, "Oh, I could tell you boys some wonderful things, only you ain't got nothin' to put it in yet."

"Coming within an understanding distance of God," and "getting something to put it in" are what prayer is about.

Finally, something should be said about "giving hands and feet to our prayers." Cultivation of prayer is not just cerebral. Harry Emerson Fosdick liked to say that prayer is love on its knees. This suggests that prayer is not just getting an answer *from* God; it is also a matter of being an answer *for* God.

The Reverend Kip Wolfe, minister of the First Christian Church in Wichita Falls, Texas, tells of being in St. Louis, Missouri, for a national church convention during the flooding of 1993.

He says he spent a lot of time in prayer for those flood victims, and during that prayer time he received a very keen sense of what God wanted him to do. He says that God's message was very clear. It went something like this, "I have heard your tale of woe, now get your tail down to a levee and make some sandbags." And so he did.

There was an opportunity one afternoon to go on school buses with a group from the church assembly. He admits that he was afraid and even thought of the possibility that the levee might break, and he could be drowned.

But he went to the levee and spent several exhausting hours filling and moving sandbags. He felt that in some small way he helped at a very critical point of need.

He said the lesson he learned was this: "Do not pray unless you are willing to go to the river."

Prayer is not just about getting an answer from God. Part of the formula is praying in such a way that once in a while we become an answer for God. That is how Jesus lived his life.

※ ※ ※ ※

Does God Play Favorites?
– Thoughts About Prayer –
Chapter Four Questions for Study and Discussion

1. Unless we can expect some special favors, why pray?

2. What are the purposes of prayer?

3. When we pray, do we expect God to disrupt the natural order of things?

4. Did Jesus define his ministry by magic?

5. Is there a difference between magic and miracle?

6. Is it possible to build "prayer muscle?"

7. What does it mean to say, "Don't pray unless you are willing to go to the river"?

5

The Christological Problem

L ecturing at Yale Divinity School on the absolutely vital task
of preaching, Gardner Taylor, a great pastor and preacher
from New York City, said in 1976, "Seeing fire in a neighbor's
house one does not casually notify his neighbor, but rushes to
shout the warning. . . . There is a place for great intensity in
preaching . . . we deal with matters of life and death . . . idolatries
of race, region, property and nation afflict our society . . . People
are not saved by being flattered but by being opposed . . . but
opposed by one who deeply cares for them . . . there are social
words that must be spoken."

Taylor speaks of "idolatries of race, region, property and nation,"
but what about idolatries of theological perspective? And are
there not *theological* words that must be spoken? Some
Christological perspectives have tended to diminish God and separate us from those whom God also loves–that is, even our fellow
human beings. I am convinced that this has historically been so;
and when that happens, somebody needs "to shout the warning."

I will not here seek to reproduce all of Raymond Brown's careful
analysis and evaluation presented in his *An Introduction to New
Testament Christology* about the Biblical picture of Jesus' self-
perspective. Indeed, as Brown illustrates, the message is mixed.

He acknowledges that "the sayings and deeds of Jesus reported
in the Gospels have been influenced by hindsight after the resurrection" (p. 24), that, in fact, "the Gospels were written to tell
people not what Jesus thought of himself but what they should

think of Jesus." (p. 23)

But Brown does reach some conclusions about the titles applied to Jesus. For instance, about the title of "Messiah" he says, "I think it most implausible that Jesus ever denied that he was the Messiah . . . it is very probable that followers of Jesus during his lifetime confessed him as Messiah" (p.79). Brown makes it clear, however, that Jesus reshaped the content of what "Messiah" means. This certainly may explain a large part of the *secrecy* motif found especially in Mark's Gospel.

Jesus didn't want the disciples to "tell anybody" because he knew they didn't fully understand the term as he represented it. Brown describes it in this manner:

> "Is it logical to suppose that Jesus never denied he was the Messiah and yet was not enthusiastic about the title as it was proposed? One can easily imagine circumstances in which it would have been perfectly logical.
>
> For example, if Jesus considered himself as God's final agent in bringing about the kingdom, he might not have denied he was the Messiah because in the minds of many that would have signified that he was not God's final agent. On the other hand, his understanding of himself may have meant that he did not fit any previous expectation exactly, and so he could not enthusiastically affirm he was the Messiah" (p. 80).

About the *parousia* (second coming, dawn of the kingdom) Brown suspects that Jesus' own position was not clear. Certainly that is what Mark 13:32 affirms. It is one of a number of texts cited by Brown that would seem to illustrate the humanity of Jesus (limited knowledge is not thought of as a divine attribute).

One of my favorite texts, clearly drawing a line of distinction between Jesus and God and putting the emphasis on Jesus' humanity, is Mark 10:17-18–"... a man ... asked him, 'Good teacher, what must I do to inherit eternal life?' And Jesus said to him, 'Why do you call me good? No one is good but God alone.'"

My bias and concern have, I assume, become clear. I feel that our Christological tendency should be to emphasize more the humanity of Jesus and, except for John's Gospel, that is the direction of most of the New Testament.

Somewhat surprisingly, however, that is not the position reached by Brown. After recognizing that "Jesus is never called God in the Synoptic Gospels," and pointing out that "Even the Fourth Gospel never portrays Jesus as saying specifically that he is God," and showing that "The sermons that Acts attributes to the beginning of the Christian mission do not speak of Jesus as God" (p. 190), still Brown aligns himself with the early conciliar decisions.

Even after page upon page of analysis showing the relativity of the scriptures on Christological issues and with the predominance of the texts supporting an emphasis on the humanity of Jesus instead of calling Jesus God (p. 174-176), Brown declares that the Nicene Creed (true God from true God) collects the sense of the scriptures, though "not dependent on any one statement of Scripture" (p. 172).

A similar inconsistency by Brown is cited by Bishop Spong in *Born Of A Woman.* About Brown's defense of the virgin birth Spong says, "Although Professor Brown is, in my estimation, the world's leading New Testament scholar, he does not draw the inescapable conclusion required by his scholarly probing that the virgin birth is nothing but Luke's theological invention. As a Roman Catholic he must constantly discipline his scholarship in the service of the official teaching and dogma of tradition. That makes it difficult for him to follow his scholarship if it leads to

71

ecclesiastically unacceptable conclusions, or to raise critical questions that seem to point in a contrary direction" (p. 124).

Now why am I rushing "to shout the warning"? Am I serious in suggesting that those who say Jesus is God are committing a kind of idolatry? Even though I respect and honor their sincerity and their scholarship, yes, I must oppose their conclusions. But I oppose them as one who deeply cares, believing that we have waited too long to challenge the ancient creeds along some very Biblical lines. Why? Because the Biblical images of Christ offer greater dimension and are more translatable to our own time, culture and world-view.

I am aware that there are several Christological titles used in the New Testament (including Messiah, Son of God, Son of Man, Lord), and they all have meaning and legitimacy. I affirm them.

I know there are different *moments* in the Gospels and in Paul when Jesus' Sonship (Christological stature) is either affirmed by the disciples or established by God. For Paul, the earliest New Testament writer, that moment seems to be the resurrection (Romans 1:4). For Mark, the earliest Gospel writer, that moment is Jesus' baptism (Mark 1:10-11). So between Paul and Mark the *moment* moves from Easter to Baptism "*but,*" says Spong in *Rescuing the Bible from Fundamentalism*, "in both instances it was the work of the Spirit" (p. 216). That is, there is something mysterious and wondrous here–a sense of special calling, enlistment and authorization by God being affirmed.

The *Spirit* continues to be the active agent in Matthew and Luke, but for them the *moment* moves from baptism to conception. It remains for John's Gospel, the latest written, to suggest that even conception was not soon enough to identify Jesus with the pre-existent Word of God.

I have no problem with the variety of titles or of moments. These, to me, represent legitimate and meaningful interpretive differences, each with its own richness of metaphorical impact.

It is, at times, difficult, even confusing, to have four portraits of Jesus, as in the four Gospels, or even five when you include Paul, but the early church went with the difficulty, or confusion, of multiplicity in order to have fullness and richness. They would not settle for the homogenizing of Tacian and his "Diateseron" or "collated gospel."

For instance, in the Passion narratives we have three different *portraits* of Jesus (Matthew-Mark, Luke and John). But as Krister Stendahl pointed out in *The Art of Preaching* (1984 Beecher Lecture), "When we have three different pictures of a loved one, we don't make transparencies and put them one on top of the other. Rather, we look at them separately and lovingly."

So I have no problem with the Christological shadings suggested by the various titles or different moments of announcement or recognition. Even John's identification between the preexistent Word of God and Jesus is rich with meaning as it affirms that the "intentionality of God" was powerfully expressed in the human Jesus.

This, in my understanding, is not the same as equating Jesus with God. In fact, it guards against that. It was the "Word" that "was in the beginning" with God–not Jesus. Then the Word became enfleshed in Jesus.

So, with reasonable, interpretive latitude I have no problem with the Christological shadings suggested by the various titles or different moments of announcement or recognition.

My critiques of the Christological journey historically, especially from 200-500 A.D., and the continuing support of those early conciliar decisions through a frozen definition of "orthodoxy" are outlined in the following:

1)   It has tended to undermine the "sense of the scriptures" by claiming for Jesus what he seems to have refused to claim for himself–that is, equality with God. Thus the second through the fourth centuries of conciliar pronouncements, rather than the scriptures themselves, became the spectacles through which Christological affirmations were made.

For example, Brown, in tracing the usage of the title "God" for Jesus says, "a title that according to the available evidence he did not use of himself and is not attested of him during the early decades of Christianity" (p.107).

Three texts are especially illustrative. They are Mark 10:18, "Why do you call me good? No one is good but God alone," and John 14:28, "for the Father is greater than I." This latter is an important balance in John's Gospel because other texts in John do sometimes shade the distinction between Jesus and God. Then there is the Christological/doxological hymn in Philippians 2:5-9:

> *"Have this mind among yourselves, which you have in Christ Jesus, who, though he was in the form of God, did not count equality with God a thing to be grasped, but emptied himself, taking the form of a servant, being born in the likeness of men. And being found in human form he humbled himself and became obedient unto death, even death on a cross. Therefore God has highly exalted him and bestowed on him the name which is above every name, that at the name of Jesus every knee should bow, in heaven, and on earth and under the earth, and every tongue confess that Jesus Christ is Lord, to the glory of God the Father."*

This hymn may not have originally been from the pen of Paul, but he uses it affirmatively and confessionally. I quote it in full in order to make several interpretive comments.

Some have seen this as proof of Paul's exaltation of Jesus to equality with God, at the least a statement of *high* Christology. I think not. I believe it is a very balanced or *moderate* Christological statement. If the metaphor of preexistence is used, which this text does, it calls to mind the highly imaginative scene of the human Jesus being *in heaven* as an adult, conversing with God, perhaps as an equal, but then shrinking to become born as a baby. This is interesting imagery but highly metaphorical and poetic–not a statement of literal fact.

Still the primary thrust or *truth* is a description of the humble character of this person Jesus, who knows his appropriate relationship to God–that is, "not counting equality with God a thing to be grasped." Why, then, has some of the church continued to *grasp* for him what he refused to *grasp* for himself?

Yes, God exalted him, and at his name every knee should bow, not to the glory of Jesus, but "to the glory of God the Father." The hymn affirms a distinction between Father and Son. Jesus can embody and convey the purposes of God, but according to this text, Jesus is not God. And Paul's counsel is that the kind of mind we should have among ourselves (in the church) is the kind of mind exemplified in Jesus who did *not* grasp at equality with God.

2)   The second problem with the historical trend of Christology is that it has tended to encourage superstition, literalizing for the popular mind what I believe should be understood as metaphorical and poetic. We cannot *know* the ontological diagram of the being of God, and surely that is not what faith is all about anyway. Remember, we have said that faith is not "the uncritical acceptance of the unbelievable but trusting that certain characteristics are what God is like and living by them," more a matter of relationship than content of belief.

So, the emphasis on the trinitarian formula, the emphasis on the virgin birth and literalizing the words of Jesus in John's Gospel have sometimes encouraged Christianity to be practiced as form without substance. This has contributed to self-righteous sectarianism and diminished the size of the Christian vision.

Bishop Spong in the last chapter of *Rescuing the Bible from Fundamentalism*, "Who Is Christ For Us?" makes much the same point: " . . . these creeds did . . . change the biblical images dramatically. The question is never, 'Who is Christ?' as if there were some pure objective human capacity to capture truth for all time. The question is, 'Who is Christ for us?' How do we as subjects carried along in the stream of history, whether we are conscious of it or not, apprehend the reality of Jesus and appropriate that reality for our time?"

Continuing to describe the efforts of the "framers of the creeds," he says, "They dealt with words that the original Jewish Christians could not have fathomed. Far more than the church fathers recognized, they were moving the Christ experience far beyond its original vocabulary" (p. 229). And I would add, far beyond its original intent.

The confusion generated by a one-dimensional literalism combined with an outmoded metaphysics (i.e., one set in the language forms of a bygone era) is clearly illustrated in the Nicene Creed.

The problem is at least three-fold:

a) The word "creed," suggesting an unswerving *this I believe*, invites an overly literal understanding.

b) The imagery is often spatial and based on the assumption of a three-story universe. John A. T. Robinson underscored this problem in his provocative little book, *Hon-

est to God, three decades ago. It should still be required reading in every adult Sunday School class. We no longer believe that *hell* is *down there, literally* somewhere near the center of the earth, or surely it would have been excavated and air-conditioned by now. And *heaven* is not literally *up there*, or our satellite systems and space probes would have disrupted some celestial prayer meeting.

When a five-year old boy asks his father "Do rockets kill God?" it is obvious that we live in a different age than that which framed the Nicene Creed.

In fact, the Roman Catholics' persecution of Galileo was based on being "stuck" in the creedal imagery used in a literalistic manner.

c)   Dependence on outmoded and archaic word forms tends to freeze the faith journey into a straightjacket of literalism. Orthodoxy based on the Nicene Creed (literally understood) tries unfruitfully to present a living, dynamic God through the vehicle of a *dead* language.

This is why Alexander Campbell suggested 150 years ago that the Bible itself should be retranslated for every generation.

The Nicene Creed is presented here in its entirety for reference and illustration.

Nicene Creed

We believe in one God,
the Father, the Almighty,
maker of heaven and earth,
of all that is, seen and unseen.

We believe in one Lord, Jesus Christ,
    the only Son of God,
    eternally begotten of the Father,
    God from God, Light from Light,
    true God from true God,
    begotten, not made,
    of one Being with the Father.
    Through him all things were made.
For us and for our salvation
    he came down from heaven,
was incarnate of the Holy Spirit and the Virgin
    Mary and became truly human.
For our sake he was crucified under Pontius
    Pilate; he suffered death and was buried.
On the third day he rose again
    in accordance with the Scriptures;
he ascended into heaven
    and is seated at the right hand of the Father.
He will come again in glory
    to judge the living and the dead,
    and his kingdom will have no end.
We believe in the Holy Spirit, the Lord
    the giver of life,
    who proceeds from the Father and the Son,
    who with the Father and the Son
    is worshiped and glorified,
    who has spoken through the prophets.

We believe in the one holy catholic (universal)
    and apostolic church.
We acknowledge one baptism
    for the forgiveness of sins.
We look for the resurrection of the dead,
    and the life of the world to come. Amen.

Set in a service of worship in a Gothic cathedral with a deeply faithful people intoning the words as their symbolic enactment of rootedness in a great tradition that has always tried to point to God's love manifested in Jesus Christ–that is a beautiful thing. But as a literal guide to the *facts of faith* and what one ought to believe, it is sorely lacking.

3)   The historical equation of Jesus with God compromises a monotheistic faith stance and makes interfaith dialogue more difficult in our religiously pluralistic society. It creates a *superiority complex* that tends to make some Christians less than Christian in demeanor when they address people of a different faith persuasion.

Again Spong expresses a similar concern: "The time has come, in my opinion, for all religious systems, including Christianity, to look at the truth that lies beneath the words of every great world religion, to respect that truth, to learn from that truth and to spend its missionary efforts only on those lives that have no sense of the holy, no experience of a transcendent wonder" (p.171 –*Rescuing the Bible from Fundamentalism*).

4)   The historical trend in Christianity in emphasizing the divinity of Jesus over his humanity, and then taking the further step of saying that Jesus is God, does not do full honor to the awesomeness of God's grace and love for human beings.

Here I must quote at length from Brown in order to challenge his conclusion. He says in the concluding chapter of *An Introduction to New Testament Christology*, "Once, after a lecture I gave on Jesus as God in the New Testament, a student asked me why the issue of full divinity raised at Nicea was so important. What difference does it make whether Jesus was God or the most perfect creature, so long as one has accepted him as Savior? Behind such a question there is often the suspicion that Nicaea and Chalcedon and indeed all the Christological controversies of the 4th and 5th centuries were matters of diphthongs (for those who know the history, Homoousians vs. Homoiousians) and of by-gone metaphysics that have no relevance today. I could not dis-agree more; for I think the issue of the full identity of Jesus, which is related to the insights of Nicaea and Chalcedon, is ultimately a question of the love of God for human beings."

"If Jesus is not 'true God of true God,' then we do not know God in human terms . . . A god who sent a marvelous creature as our Saviour could be described as loving, but that love would have cost God nothing in a personal way. Only if Jesus is truly of God do we know that God's love was so real that it reached the point of personal self-giving" (p.150-151).

Four observations:

a) Brown dodges or misses the point when he switches from saying "Jesus is God" to "Jesus is *of* God." The preposition does matter and suggests some distinction be-tween God and Jesus and suggests, I believe, that Jesus is not God. I like the phrase "Jesus is *of* God."

b) To say that it costs God nothing in a personal way unless Jesus is *of* God really begs the question. Aren't we all "*of* God"? Doesn't it *cost God* something *in a per-sonal way* when any of his creation is distorted, injured or destroyed?

c) Granted that Jesus is *of* God in a special and unique way as in, for instance, "Son of God"–for I believe and affirm that–isn't the same as saying "Jesus *is* God."

d) Most importantly, Brown's position misses the power of John 3:16-17 when he asserts that Jesus is God. To risk oneself is not as costly in a personal way as to risk one's child. Speaking as a parent and grandparent, I can affirm that the contemplation of the loss of my own life is not nearly so awesome as the contemplation of the loss of my child's or grandchild's life. Risking one's son, and having one's son willing to take the risk, is more awesome, more personally costly, than risking oneself.

5) Historically the weight has tended to be so much on the divinity of Jesus as to make the life, suffering and death of Jesus seem like play acting. Jesus means much more to me if I feel that he really shared the fullness of what it means to be human, warts and all. Let me illustrate the problem.

A deserving young man went to work one Monday morning in the lowest position in a huge manufacturing plant. His starting salary was only ten dollars a day, but determinedly he began his climb up the ladder. Inside a month he was head of the shipping department and making five hundred a week. Two months later he was running the sales force and earning a thousand a week. And exactly one year after his humble start the owner called him in and said, "Young man, you've done well. You are hereby named president of the company at two hundred thousand a year."

"Thank you," said the young man.

"Thank you, he tells me," grumbled the boss. "Haven't you anything else to say for yourself?"

"Yes," said the young man, "Please tell Mom I won't be home for dinner." If Jesus is God or at least genetically *special*, then his earthly life cannot be quite *real* for us.

This, of course, is the problem with the doctrine of the virgin birth. It effectively denies the essential humanity of Jesus, turning him into a strange visitor from another planet and separating him from human experience as we know it.

The surprising thing is that even a cursory view of scriptural material reveals that this doctrine is not the majority position of the Bible. It does not reflect "the sense of the scriptures."

Matthew's reference (Matthew 1:22-25) is based on a mistranslation in the Septuagint (an early Greek translation of the Hebrew Scriptures) of Isaiah 7:14 which in the original Hebrew referred to "a young maiden," not "a virgin."

Luke, for his own reasons, adopts the idea and then builds a whole Christmas pageant on this error, emphasizing his sense of Jesus' specialness in a way that ultimately separates Jesus from real human life. There were many virgin birth claims current in that time, and Luke must have wanted Jesus to have all the trappings of any other hero.

However, none of the other three major writers in the New Testament reference it and their silence alone should diminish its importance. But more than their silence we should also attend to *when* they wrote, positive references to Joseph as Jesus' father (one of which even occurs in Luke 4:22), and the genealogies in Matthew 1 and Luke 3 which trace Jesus' lineage through Joseph.

The two earliest writers, Paul and Mark, reflect no virgin birth tradition. And John's gospel, the last written, gives it no attention and specifically refers to Joseph as Jesus' father twice, John 1:45 and 6:42. It seems that it was important to John to clarify Jesus' natural origins. Perhaps by the time he wrote he was consciously contending against Luke's version. Again, the Bible is not one-dimensional.

Scripturally this doctrine is not well supported and Christologically it makes Jesus less real in human terms, therefore less meaningful for people approaching the 21st century.

One final word of clarification in defining "The Christological problem." It is important to acknowledge the difference between the Jesus of history and the post-resurrection Christ of faith.

Marcus Borg in *Meeting Jesus Again for the First Time* says, "There simply is a major difference between what Jesus was like as a figure of history and how he is spoken of in the gospels and later Christian tradition." (p. 15) Borg uses the terms "the pre-Easter Jesus" and "the post-Easter Jesus" to designate this distinction.

Most of the Biblical record is about the pre-Easter Jesus, though the Biblical presentations of Jesus have certainly been colored, shaded, nuanced in retrospective ways by the resurrection faith of the writers of the New Testament. So the New Testament pictures are not simply historical; they are *interpreted history*–that is, history infused with meaning.

We are not able to get an unclouded portrait of the pre-Easter Jesus, and yet we believe that the one we experience as the post-Easter Jesus and what we mean when we give content to the pre-existent Word as in John's prologue *are both dependent on the Jesus of history*.

Jesus, the man, did live in time and space as we know it. He may even have sinned. How shall we define the term? Certainly he knew desolation and loneliness. He knew what it meant to feel forsaken, denied, betrayed. He struggled with temptation. Was he always victorious? We do not know. What we do know in faith and according to the Biblical witness is that his life was worthy to be called "Son of God." We do not know whether that sonship can be defined ontologically in physicalistic terms from the *genetics* of God in pre-history or not. Probably not. That is not what the prologue of John's Gospel means to me.

I do believe that, *spiritually speaking,* Jesus was an expression of the intentionality of God about the direction and purpose of human life and that this *intentionality* was always part of God's being.

The resurrection is God's "YES" to the life of the historical Jesus, to how it expressed the *intentionality of God*.

It is my belief that Jesus became *Son of God, Messiah, Son of Man, Lord, Savior* because of the quality of his life and his relationship to God.

Others would contend (Brown often uses the term "God's plan") that a script had been written at the dawn of history that included the arrival of the *Messiah* at the *right time*. As many have pointed out, this was *kairos* time, not *chronos* time–a time of spiritual readiness, not to be confused with the chronology of calendar time.

Jesus did come at the right *kairos* but not as a matter of the spinning out of some foreordained drama. Rather it became the right time because of the quality of Jesus' life, obedience and faith and a certain readiness on the part of a needy world.

Jesus fulfilled not a *plan* but a *hope* in the heart of God. Otherwise God becomes no more than a grand puppeteer, and Jesus danced at his bidding with no real choices to make. Most rational and faithful people in the century to come will not believe that and will not want to live life under that metaphor, because to do so robs the human endeavor of real seriousness.

How then shall we *nuance* our language in talking about Jesus so that the "Christological problem" becomes less fuzzy as we enter the 21st century? How can the tone and shadings of our remarks make more clear to others how Jesus is "God's man" rather than continuing to cling to the imagery of a superhuman "Godman" masquerading as a human being?

◈ The Christology Problem ◈
Chapter Five Questions for Study and Discussion

1. Is it possible for a person to be idolatrous in his/her theological perspective?

2. Do you think Jesus thought of himself as Messiah? What will have shaped his "messianic" expectations?

3. Do you think Jesus thought he was the same as God?

4. What are the different *moments* when the different New Testament authors affirm Jesus' special relationship to God? Is one *right* and are the others *wrong*?

5. Do you have certain characteristics of one of your parents? Do you remind people of one of your parents? Are you the same person as one of your parents?

6. Which causes the greatest sense of loss, the contemplation of your own death or the contemplation of the death of your child or grandchild?

7. If the scripts of life (whether Jesus' or yours or mine) have already been written, what happens to the idea of responsibility?

→ Don Alexander

6

Nuancing Our Language About Jesus Christ

First, a brief confessional and historical overview:

"Messiah" in Greek is "Christos." The essential meaning of the term is "anointed one." When I make my confession of faith that Jesus is the Christ, the son of the living God, I am affirming: 1) Jesus' special relationship to God; 2) Jesus being other than God (someone was anointed and someone did the anointing, someone is son and someone is father); and 3) a sense of mission. Jesus is anointed or appointed to a task, the reinstitution of *God's rule* in people's lives.

The "Messianic hope" is a specification (though not the only one) of how God's rule of justice, peace and love will come into being.

Historically this *hope* became associated with the Davidic line of kingship in Hebrew culture. In the Old Testament the ruling king of Israel was generally called "the anointed of Yahweh (God)." It is not surprising that the name "Messiah" eventually transferred to the ideal king of the future.

In Jewish and in Christian thought the messianic expectation is linked with the world of ideas which surrounded the historic Davidic kingship. This especially came to flower during the Babylonian captivity following the fall of Jerusalem in 587 B.C. Then again during the Hasmonean dynasty from about 165-55 B.C., prior to Roman domination and the reign of Herod the Great, this concept resurfaced.

This *messianic hope* gained focus during the Babylonian captivity because it provided a golden age to remember and idealize. Then during the Hasmonean dynasty (reign of the Maccabees) the image was heightened because the party not in power was always idealized. The Davidic line still existed, and it was known who would have been crowned. But the Maccabees were in control–levying taxes, making arrests and issuing mandates so the Davidic line could bask in the glow of idealized memory.

What is the nature of these idealized *kingly* characteristics? The king provides for law and justice in the land; he secures for his people the blessings of God; he defeats all enemies; and he will rule forever over the whole world. These characteristics are seen in the *Royal Psalms* (Psalms 2, 18, 20, 21, 45, 72, 101, 110, 132).

Originally these Psalms were in praise of the present king, but they came to be transferred to the future-oriented belief in the "Messiah yet to come." Thus, for example, Acts 4:25 can use Psalm 2 as a reference to Jesus, though it was not originally so intended.

Other *messianic* features other than kingly ones are drawn from Isaiah and Micah and were probably poetic references to an *original man* image that evolved out of a mix of Jewish thinking and near Eastern myths. Characteristics included in this mix were the origin of the Messiah in primitive time, his mysterious birth, eating milk and honey (known elsewhere as "food for the gods") and his being the deliverer of the peace of paradise.

The Jews practiced a strict monotheism. We must remember that in the expectations of the future in the Hebrew scriptures, the Messiah always plays only a subordinate role–more a *symbol* and a *gift* of the time of salvation ushered in by Yahweh himself (Isaiah 2:4 and Isaiah 9:6). The effecting of the change is not really the task of the Messiah. He is the representative or instrument of Yahweh. In Isaiah 52:7, for instance, Yahweh himself is the king at the time of salvation.

On the other hand the prophets have cognizance of various instruments which God uses to achieve his plan of salvation. (Isaiah 44:28 speaks of Cyrus, a foreign king–"He is my shepherd and he shall fulfill all my purpose.") In Isaiah 45:1 Yahweh even addresses Cyrus as "his anointed."

"Suffering Servant of God" and "Son of Man" images were brought into synthesis with the figure of the Messiah only in New Testament times. A Messiah who suffers and dies as a substitute for all men in the New Testament sense was only dimly foreshadowed in Judaism–the "suffering servant" of Isaiah, for instance.

Jesus then, as presented in creedal formulations, was not so much the fulfillment of the Messianic Hope of Jewish thought as something of a reshaping or new specification of that image.

In fact, Jesus refuses to be seen in the kingly role in any political sense. Although he is pictured as prophesying suffering and death for himself, it is not so much as a substitute for "sinful man" as it is a *sign* of the intentionality of God working through him. And so I believe the interpretive emphasis should be on Jesus Christ not as a "sacrificial lamb," but as "God's ambassador of love." And if the interpretive emphasis is on Jesus Christ as "sacrificial lamb," then we must deal with that concept in terms of its Hebrew origins, a sign from God rather than a price paid to God in exchange for forgiveness or release from bondage.

We continue to reframe it–the Christological problem–that is, how should we as Christians present (talk about) Jesus Christ to others? How can we present Jesus to the world in ways most consistent with his own sense of purpose and mission? What did his disciples believe that he was about? How was he understood by the early church (especially 200-500 A.D.)? How should we, in the light of the Biblical message of salvation, shape our Christology for the 21st century? What about the relationship between the Jesus of history and the Christ of the resurrection faith?

We have affirmed the function of religion in our lives. It should provide a connection or reconnection to all that can give meaning, shape and fullest dimension to our living.

And we have conveyed deep appreciation for the Bible. It contains a growing understanding of what God is like, and what by God's help we are to become. We see the Bible as true, yet still retain some reservations about how the Bible has been misused.

I hope I have provided some helpful perspective on God as Creator, Judge and Redeemer, the source and resource for all of life.

Now we must ask, what part does Jesus play in all of this?

How important, how essential (that is, "part of the essence") is Jesus Christ in our individual lives, to the life of the church and for the salvation of the world? Surely for the Christian the answers will be different from what persons of other faiths might say, but the Christian's answers need not be polarizing or categorically exclusive.

I want to express deep appreciation to Raymond E. Brown, the Roman Catholic New Testament scholar, for his very thorough scriptural analysis in *An Introduction to New Testament Christology;* to John Shelby Spong, the Episcopal bishop, for his books *Rescuing the Bible from Fundamentalism* and *Born of a Woman;* to Fred B. Craddock for his *Commentary on John* and *Overhearing the Gospel;* to Marcus Borg for his biographical journey of faith in *Meeting Jesus Again for the First Time;* and to

Gil Bailie for his very helpful insights on the meaning of the crucifixion in *Violence Unveiled.*

Though they take different approaches and reach varied conclusions, they all exhibited a spirit of openness to the interpretive process and helped me tremendously in shaping my understanding of the dimensions of "the Christological problem." I would recommend these volumes to lay and clergy alike as being most readable and succinct.

Then I must acknowledge Thomas Oden who initially refocused my attention on Christological concerns, though in a negative way. The flavor of his remarks in *After Modernity . . . What? Agenda For Theology,* a 1990 revision of an earlier book, surfaced a negative reaction on my part to some of his basic assumptions, assumptions certainly that are not his alone. Let me here review the assertions that prompted my adverse responses and that will provide further direction for our Christological inquiry.

Most disturbing are two sweeping assumptions:

1)   The acceptance and promotion by Oden and others of the first one thousand years of church history as defining *orthodoxy* (right teaching). The endorsement of the consensual position of the church councils of the first millenium as being more normative than the scriptures themselves for defining orthodoxy I find objectionable. I felt this tendency somewhat in Raymond Brown, but Brown is more careful to leave open the doors and windows of the dialogic process between what the Bible says (in all its diversity) and how the early church interpreted the Biblical content.

The early church *interpretations,* as represented in the decisions of the early councils (for instance, Nicea in 325 A.D. and Chalcedon in 451 A.D.), tended to build on the Gospel of John's "logos" theology and to equate Jesus with God (true God and true man). There is a tendency to think that this solves all issues in Christology (I felt that to be Oden's position). However, Brown keeps the door open when he says, "In particular, many Roman Catholics are shocked to learn that their church, although insisting that its dogmas articulate revealed truth, has recognized the historical conditioning, and, hence, the limitation of dogmatic formulations" (p. 147).

It is this historical conditioning that requires comment. In retrospect it seems to me that the equation of Jesus with God is not the "sense of the scriptures" as suggested by Brown and other Roman Catholics and consistently maintained by Oden. The early church fathers were themselves prisoners of their world-view and culture, *even as are we all to some degree.*

I would contend that, being in the formative stages of "establishing the faith" and living with a world-view that tended to define in supernatural categories what could not be explained otherwise, they overemphasized the ontological *specialness* of Jesus in order to assert and establish the authority of the church.

But this becomes, I believe, contrary to the scripture's presentation of how the disciples saw Jesus and of how Jesus seems to have understood himself and his mission. The definitions of early church councils were too much on Jesus' divinity and equality with God, and their dogma tended to solidify into a one-dimensional view.

Is *orthodoxy* to be represented best by the assertions of the early councils *or* by an ongoing reinterpretation of the words of Jesus? For instance, "the sabbath was made for man, not man for the sabbath" (Mark 2:27) might be paraphrased to read "dogma was made for man, not man for dogma." And perhaps Jesus' words, "you have heard that it was said of old, but I say to you" (Matthew 5:21, 27), may be understood as his reinterpretation, rephrasing, redefining or updating of the orthodoxy of his own day. And surely in his response in Mark 10:18, "Why do you call me good? No one is good but God alone," Jesus clearly pronounces a *distinction from* rather than an *equation with* God.

Orthodoxy should be understood as dynamic rather than static. It is evolving and emerging; written, if you please, on the heart rather than on tablets of stone, not frozen in time but evolving into each new age.

2)   The second negative motivator was Oden's unbending emphasis on what he calls "the theandric man" concept and trinitarian dogma as being normative for all future Christological discussion. He says, "Historical inquiry into Jesus . . . will not begin until the premise of theandric union . . . is taken as a serious hypothesis for exegetes" (p.103). He sums up his Christological bias with this definition: " . . . the rudiments of classic Christian teaching–trinity and theandric union in the person of Christ" (p. 117).

There is a presumptuousness, an arrogance and a triumphalist (salvation only in Jesus) tone in this kind of language that seems to almost rule out any dialogic or interpretive process. Certainly it is not reflective of the tone of most of the New Testament witness.

For instance, the language Jesus most used about himself and that the disciples used about him clearly assumed a distinction between Jesus and God, stressing Jesus' humanity rather than divinity. Even the most used terms in the New Testament– "Christ," "Son of God," "Son of Man"–express *distinction from* rather than *the same as* and imply *specialness* but certainly not *equality with God*.

I am aware of the "I am" statements in John's Gospel and the strong possibility that they should be interpreted in the light of the great "I AM" in Exodus 3:14, drawing a strong, unifying circle around Jesus and God. Also, the writer in John includes Jesus' affirmation in prayer to God, "even as we are one" (John 17:11). But then, again in John's Gospel, Jesus prays that his followers may be in them (God and Jesus) as they are in each other (John 17:21). This certainly should not be read to mean that we become *the same as* God or that we are God's equal. Concurrently, there is the statement from Jesus' mouth in John 14:28, "for the Father is greater than I." Indeed, the Bible is not one-dimensional.

Having critiqued some assumptions about orthodoxy and dogma that seem contrary to the spirit of the scriptures, I hope it will be helpful at this point to discuss the appropriate *nuancing* of the language we use to talk about Jesus Christ under some specifically descriptive headings:

1) As with most cautions, this first is *easier said than done*. But I believe we should, as much as possible, present our convictions of faith in common, everyday language. A phrase like "unique theandric man" seems a presumptuous clouding of Jesus' humanity and tends to cast a haze of unapproachability over how Jesus is related to God.

Too often the language of theological discourse clouds and confuses rather than simplifies and clarifies. The phrase "unique theandric man" literally means "one of a kind, godman man."

I am reminded of the sarcastic grade school patter, "I perceive that your diction is too opaque for my Lilliputian understanding. You will therefore be compelled to elucidate and clarify your harangue of all polysyllabic verbifications." The language we use to talk about life's most important issues should be as clear and straightforward as possible.

2) Christological assertions are metaphorical. That is, when we

talk about the preexistence of Christ, which passages in John encourage us to do (John 1:1 and 17:5), or when we speak of the Trinity (God being one, but having three expressions through which God is encountered), we are talking metaphorically. We are using "word images" to describe a reality that we really cannot know, but we think this a helpful way to talk about the fullness of God's being. The church has traditionally used images of the preexistence of Christ and the Trinity to describe what God is like.

Personally I find these meaningful *with interpretation* but not exhaustive. They are not the only, and perhaps not even the most helpful, ways to describe God and Jesus and how they are related.

For instance, Oden says that "the story of God's own coming . . . cannot be narrated without the theandric premise" and "The uncreated One assumed the life of creature" (p. 131-132). Then when he anchors these assertions by paraphrasing John's Gospel that "The Word became flesh in a person in history," he may be forcing John's prologue into a straight jacket of arrogance.

This is the crux of my critique of Oden. I believe that the story of God's own coming can be narrated without the "theandric" or "Godman" premise and, in fact, that it has been so narrated in much of the New Testament. John's prologue is more of a theological than a Christological statement—telling what God is like and one of the ways in which God is known in the world.

And, of course, how we understand "Word" in John's prologue is crucial. If "Word" means or is equivalent to God, John could have simply said, "God became flesh and dwelt among us"? But if "Word" will bear other weight (as indeed I believe it will), such as *expression of God, wisdom of, purposiveness of, energy of* or *intentionality of*, then I see John drawing a common sense distinction between Jesus and God, yet still making a strong affirmation about how one expresses the other. To say that Jesus is "God's man," a purposive expression of the intentionality and energy of God is not the same as saying, "Jesus is God." Some have suggested that Trinity be seen as a *functional* image rather than an *ontological* one–that is, more a description of how we come to experience God rather than a description of "how God is."

William Barclay in his commentary on John's prologue offers further clarification about the phrase "the Word was God." Barclay suggests that the Greek usage of the definite article "ho theos" speaks of God as a noun, but when, in Greek, the definite article is not used, it becomes more of an adjectival usage. This is the case here. When John said "the Word was God" he was not saying that Jesus was *identical* with God but that Jesus was God-like," revealing the nature and essential qualities of God.

In a common sense sort of way (whether intended or not) the church's dogma about Jesus and God has tended to be understood as equational rather than incarnational, but Barclay's interpretation is more incarnational.

In Craddock's *Commentary on John,* he makes the helpful observation that the thrust of John's prologue is "not a doctrinal statement in which an understanding of God is used to explain who Jesus Christ is. Rather, the experience of Jesus was for the Johannine church an experience of God" (p. 9–notice he does not say THE experience of God).

When this more experiential or confessional, rather than doctrinal, note is sounded, it removes the presumptuous overtones that I hear in "Godman" and Trinitarian pronouncements.

3)   This points the way to a third observation as we nuance our Christological language: it should be confessional in nature, not coercive.

In a general way it can be said that much of the Biblical witness is confessional language, not intended as courtroom legalese. This is specifically true in Christological affirmations. We are not to use affirmations about Jesus as a battering ram to force others to accept our doctrinal position. Invitation and not coercion is the business of the Christian. Certainly there is a place for exhortation, trying to convince or sway another to our point of view, but we must guard carefully our tone so that we do not become "un-Christian" in our efforts to persuade.

In "The Art of Preaching," Krister Stendahl's Beecher Lectures at Yale Divinity School in 1984, Stendahl suggested that the confessional language of the Bible is *love language,* and love language is not the language of the courtroom.

He said that he had often *confessed* his love to his wife in the language of love which is indeed *one and only* language. "Dear, you're the most wonderful woman in the world. I could never love another as much as I love you. " That's the language of love. It has a certain *exclusive* quality about it.

But, said Stendahl, if he had been put on the stand in a court of law and asked to swear that if he had never met and loved and married his wife that he might not have met and married another woman whom he would have loved and treasured as much as he loved and treasured his wife, he could not so swear. There is a distinction between the language of love (confessional language) and the language of the courtroom (legal language).

Two New Testament texts come to mind. They are Acts 4:12 and John 14:6.

Acts 4:12 says, "And there is salvation in no one else, for there is no other name under heaven given among men by which we must be saved." And John 14:6, "Jesus said to him, 'I am the way, and the truth, and the life; no one comes to the Father, but by me.'"

The exclusive tone of such texts is at least moderated by an understanding of the distinction between *confessional* language and the *legalese* of the court.

Both texts can be read as the confessional affirmations of the authors that Jesus was the "one and only" FOR THEM. In their passion for Jesus their language becomes exclusive in ways that Jesus himself would not have endorsed.

Craddock points to the presence of language that is *confessional* in nature in John's prologue (John 1:1-18) and suggests that this *confessional* tone is signaled by the introduction of the words *we* and *us* into the text. "As we will notice throughout the Gospel," says Craddock, "the signs and speeches of Jesus are followed by doubt and faith, confusion and understanding. Whoever would confess faith must have the courage to do so amid questioning, disagreement, rejection, or even ridicule. Faith does not wait for a majority vote" (p. 9).

Confessional language is very personal and should invite, rather than coerce. Faith can be urged but not forced. Confessional language is more experiential and, therefore, more subjective. I can confess what I have experienced without having the right to generalize. Just because an Eskimo lives in a house of ice does not mean that all people everywhere should live in igloos.

And so, although I believe that our Christological language should be confessional, we must be cautious that it not be coercive. We must make it clear to ourselves and to others that in the confessional context a thing can be true without being universal.

A spirit of inclusive humility becomes the moderating presence that protects our confessional language from becoming coercive and/or triumphalist.

4)   But Christological affirmations are not just confessional.

Often they do seem to have a polemical or argumentative tone.

Acts 4:12, for instance, appears to have been spoken to non-be-lievers, a Jewish audience. It was intended to convince the lis-tener and to work a change of mind and heart, to carve out space for a new religious perspective.

And Craddock says that in John's prologue two other communi-ties of faith are referred to, and the writer, by his confession, seeks to sway them. "The writer acknowledges that both John the Baptist and the Mosaic law are from God, but at the same time insists that there is in Jesus Christ not only a unique revela-tion of the unseen God but an offer of grace and truth. Such is the character of this Gospel's polemic: not an emotional denial of any Divine source for the other faiths, but neither an easy em-brace of everything under the guise of generous ecumenism" (p.10). Craddock says that the message is clear–"it makes a dif-ference what you believe" (p.11).

I would agree. Of course it makes a difference what you believe. And so we must ask, in terms of approach, what is the "sense of the scriptures"? Did Jesus himself *force* belief or *invite* it? Was he one-dimensional and rigid in his approach to *the tradition* or more of a contextualist, responding differently to different situa-tions? If we believe the latter is what Jesus was like, then how should we respond?

5)   Finally, of course, Christological language is theological. The root and reason for talking about Jesus Christ is to say more clearly what we believe God is like. This is not to make the equation that Jesus is God. That is not what I am saying and I hope not what the church has meant to say, but too heavy an emphasis on Nicea often makes it seem that way.

I do believe that Jesus is the one who, for us as Christians and for many others as well, "puts a face on God." We see in him the essence or intentionality of God expressed in human form–the Word made flesh. But I also want to guard against a kind of historical hocus-pocus where the preexistent Word, the intentionality of God, is equated with a historical man named Jesus from Nazareth of Galilee who existed *as God from the beginning of or even prior to creation.*

John's prologue says, "the Word *became* flesh" (emphasis mine)– the fleshly Jesus did not exist as a real human being prior to his birth.

Our Christology should express the meaning and purpose that Jesus' life (words, deeds, closeness to God, suffering, death and resurrection) has come to have for us and how that impacts our understanding of what God is like and what we are to become. But for people of the 21st century to be able to receive the "good news," it should be stripped of superstition, of being explained by way of a supernatural metaphysics.

Faith is not the uncritical acceptance of the unbelievable. Faith is trusting that certain characteristics, such as those seen and clarified in Jesus Christ, are what God is like and then living out those characteristics on a daily basis.

If we see in Jesus Christ that God is gracious, accepting us even when we are unacceptable, then a response of faith will make us more gracious, more loving and more kind.

If we see that there is moral dimension in the being of God, that God has ethical expectations of human kind, then we will try to be personally more accountable and responsible.

If we see the intentionality or purposefulness of God coming more clearly into focus in the person of Jesus, then we must live in such a way (with God's help) as to give God's purposes more of a chance in our lives and in our world.

If we see in the crucifixion that it is more Godlike to meet violence with forgiveness and understanding than with violent retribution, then we will seek to disenfranchise violence as an option of response in our social systems. Part of the meaning of Jesus' death on the cross is that violence in response to what we fear is ultimately self-defeating.

Circumstances may seem to suggest that God's purposes do not stand much of a chance, yet, *in faith* we must live them out.

And so Jesus, in faith, set his face toward Jerusalem to speak and to live the good news of God's kingdom, no matter what.

Theological language may not always be Christological, but Christological language should always be theological, pointing beyond itself to a fuller understanding of what God is like. Too *high* a Christology becomes idolatrous.

The Christological problem continually refocuses itself as we present certain questions regarding the Biblical text. How did Jesus understand his mission? Did he see himself as divine? Did the disciples? What about the early church? How was Jesus' death redemptive? Did Jesus have to die on the cross? Was Jesus born to die?

Having already celebrated the necessity of the interpretive process in chapters on the Bible and on God, we reaffirm it here in specific application to nuancing our Christological language.

We want to know the *mind* and *will* of Jesus both about issues of life and about how he understood himself and his relationship to God. Surely these are of utmost importance for those who would be his disciples, for those who would earnestly seek to follow him.

We have already said that the Bible is not one-dimensional, that

101

it interprets itself, that it can express more than one point of view on seemingly similar issues. In *Overhearing the Gospel,* Craddock clarifies the ways in which the Bible interprets itself. For instance, he says that the Bible interprets itself productively, not reproductively, in order to bring the word of Jesus in the tradition to bear upon the lives of the current readers or hearers. One example might be Matthew 19:9 where the author adds "except for unchastity" when *quoting* Jesus about divorce. Mark, Luke and Paul have no such exception. How was Matthew's audience or his understanding of Jesus' intent so different that it caused him to give a more lenient response?

Also the Bible does not worry about harmonizing each message with all its other messages on that topic. "The New Testament," says Craddock, "can urge one group to become as little children and another to quit being children without feeling it must harmonize the two into one harmless and helpless exhortation. Jesus can command one candidate for discipleship to leave all other responsibilities immediately and instruct another to sit down and count the cost" (p. 67-68).

Stendahl, too, is unapologetic in his assertion that interpretation is essential to the life of faith. He says that the scripture lives by interpretation, that the history of doctrine is simply the history of Biblical interpretation.

We, individually, and the church, collectively, continue that interpretive process. The church both created and stands under the scriptures. The scriptures and the interpretive process (under the guidelines of reason, the leading of God's spirit and the gospel of grace) are our pathway into the mind and will of Jesus Christ.

But, as we have seen, a certain relativity emerges concerning our understanding of what Jesus taught and what he understood about his life and mission *and* what the disciples understood about him. We have seen that either Jesus spoke new words to new situations or that the authors of the New Testament (representatives of the early church) continued to *interpret* his mind and will for new times and new situations. We have seen the different positions on divorce in Mark 10:11-12 and Matthew 19:9, for instance, and earlier we referenced the different perspectives on Christ's return or "the end of time" reflected in Mark 9:1, 2 Peter 3:8-10 and John 5:24.

There are still those who would ignore this *relativity* emphasis with regard to certain Christological affirmations–saying, for example, that Jesus Christ is the *only* path to salvation.

They become polemical without, at the same time, remembering that our Christological language is also metaphorical and confessional. This can lead to an arrogant, triumphalist position, forgetting the relativity of the scriptures themselves on this subject.

The seemingly exclusive statement regarding salvation in Acts 4:12 is moderated by our understanding of the confessional and polemical nature of the statement, but it also must be seen in the light of Acts 10:34-35 where Peter says, "Truly I perceive that God shows no partiality, but in every nation anyone who fears him and does what is right is acceptable to him." Again, the Bible is not one-dimensional.

And John 14:6 must be interpreted in the light of John 3:16-17– "For God so loved the WORLD . . . For God sent his Son into the WORLD not to condemn the WORLD . . . but that the WORLD might be saved through him" (emphasis mine). Now I know that John 3:18 goes on to say that "those who do not believe are condemned already"–referring, I believe, to the Jewish people of John's day who did not become Christian. (Of course, it can be expanded to embrace all who do not believe in Jesus.) John 3:18 would seem to undercut John 3:16-17.

How can God both love and condemn? There is an inconsistency here caused, I believe, by John's polemical concerns. The text does not follow its own best insight–that is, the affirmation of God's love for the world–to its logical conclusion. John 3:18 must stand under the corrective of the interpretive principle of God's grace. It is not expressive of John's Gospel at its best.

Then we would also give attention to texts such as Matthew 7:21, "Not everyone who says to me, 'Lord, Lord,' shall enter the kingdom of heaven, but he who does the will of my Father who is in heaven." Here Jesus intentionally shifts the emphasis from himself as the requirement of salvation to the doing of God's will.

Or how about Paul's sweeping affirmation in Romans 11:32, "For God has consigned all men to disobedience, that he may have mercy upon all?" That is pretty inclusive.

And Luke 12:10 with the interesting distinction drawn between the Son of Man and the Holy Spirit should confound any "triumphalist" (one who believes that there is salvation *only* in Jesus Christ and that all others will be condemned). "And everyone who speaks a word against the Son of Man will be forgiven; but he who blasphemes against the Holy Spirit will not be forgiven." This text clearly suggests that the *Holy Spirit* is more central to the life of faith than the *Son of Man*.

These words from *Gulliver's Travels* are the triumphalist's creed:

> *We are the chosen few,*
> *All others will be damned.*
> *There's no room in heaven for you;*
> *We don't want heaven crammed.*

This is, in spirit, contrary to Jesus' message and purpose if we take seriously such passages as John 3:17 ("that the WORLD might be saved") and 2 Corinthians 5:19 ("God was in Christ reconciling the WORLD to himself."). Christ is not simply the possession of those who claim the name of Jesus. He functioned in the world for the sake of all God's creation.

Gil Bailie's assertion in the epilogue of *Violence Unveiled* is provocative and illustrative, "One of the many paradoxes with which Christians must wrestle is the fact that, by its very nature, a 'pro-Christian' position is antithetical to the gospel." (p. 274)

It is not that just any old faith will do. But as seen in Jesus Christ, faith is a matter of relationship and loyalty to purpose–not of doctrine. Believing the *right* things about Christ is not as important as *being in Christ* and being *Christlike*.

Remember the farmers sitting around the pot-bellied stove at the country store on a rainy day? Because of the rain everything is soaked. No one can get in the fields to work, and so there is nothing to do but sit around and "chew the fat." The *fat* being chewed this day happens to be religion. Which is best, they wonder. Have the Presbyterians got it right with that "predestinarian stuff" or maybe the Catholics (after all "confession is good for the soul") or maybe it is the Episcopalians with their exact liturgy or the Church of Christ with their certainty about themselves.

Finally, they turn to "Ol' Sam" who has not said a word–he hardly ever does. He just sits and listens and rocks, but usually when he does speak, he seems to get just the right slant.

"Well," he says, "I'll tell ya'. If'n I was takin' my wheat to the mill, when I got there the miller wouldn't ask, 'Hey, Sam, which way did ya' come? Did ya' come by the River Road or straight through town or did ya' come by the County Pike?' Naw, what he'd ask is, 'Hey, Sam, how good is your grain?'"

We now turn to the key question for this study: As we prepare to move into the 21st century, are there some definable guidelines that can suggest the shape and direction of our Christological affirmations? I would contend that there are *and* that they are in keeping with the scriptural images of the pre-Easter and the post-Easter Jesus.

❈ ❈   ❈ ❈

⊞ Nuancing Our Language About ⊞ Jesus Christ
Chapter Six Questions for Study and Discussion

1. Can you have a special relationship with someone without being identical to that person?

2. Where did the idea of *Messiah* come from?

3 .Can what is orthodox (right teaching) ever change?

4. Can you find passages in the New Testament that accept or endorse slavery? Does that make slavery acceptable today?

5. Did Jesus ever challenge the popularly held views of his day?

6. If Jesus could *set aside* sabbath rules in order to do a kindness to someone, was he practicing *situation ethics*? That is, did Jesus sometimes let human need come before a strict adherence to legal codes?

7. Why has the church sometimes "grasped" at Jesus being equal with God when Jesus did not?

8. Is it possible to be confessional without being coercive?

9. To be true must a thing be universal? i.e., Did Jesus give the same advice to or make exactly the same demands of every person he encountered?

10. What are the *ultimate purposes* of God?

11. How can a "pro-Christian" position be antithetical to the gospel?

→ Don Alexander

7

Toward a Christology for the 21st Century

In 1975 when B. Davie Napier was delivering the Beecher Lectures at Yale Divinity School under the title "Word of God, Word of Earth," he quoted at some length from a commencement address by John Fry. His words were for our time, stressing urgency and personal responsibility in the interpretive process. They have been a stimulus to me in writing this book and provide motivation for the ongoing Christological dialogue:

"I propose . . . When you walk out of here today, you really walk out on your own, and stay on your own from now on. A part of the infantilizing procedures in theological education, which I've already noted, consists of hearing the truth from Daddy who heard it from some other bigger person, who heard it from Augustine who heard it from Paul who heard it from God.

Well, what do you think? Ask that question and here's what one gets: a 20-page paper on what all the big people think. But you in your incomparable subjectivity, and all that native intelligence . . . yes, you, right there; what do you think? Was Arius right or Nicea right? Quick, now, don't go to the library. Don't look up your lecture notes. On your own tell us—what do you think? It may look like the old authority question, but it's not. It's the old Peter Pan question about staying children always, even though M.Div. and even Ph.D.

Lo, I tell you a mystery. I've known religious figures 60 years old who, when they died, could have chiseled on their tombstones these immortal words: 'Niebuhr says, Barth says, Brunner says, but Tillich says.' But what do these figures say? One doesn't know. They've never said. They will have gone from birth to death without thinking one single thought absolutely and lustily their own."

The point here is that, although we should read and listen to what others teach and preach (otherwise why this book, why Sunday morning sermons, why Beecher lectures?), the time must come when we proclaim certain opinions, positions and affirmations our own. At the opportune, proper moment, we will say, "This I believe and God help me, I'd like you to believe it too."

The ongoing interpretive process, by which we seek to relate the Biblical good news about the life, death and resurrection of Jesus Christ to our own time, will evolve into an ever-new "orthodoxy." It will proceed by bringing to bear the traditions of the church, our own reason and experience and staying open and sensitive to the leading of God's spirit.

Here, then, are guidelines that I believe to be in tune with God's energy at work in the world and with directions suggested by an overall "sense of the scriptures." It is important to inquire about the origins of these categories. Are they indigenous to Christianity or imported from other value centers? I believe they are Christ-spirited, though they may also have found expression in and through other traditions.

As we have already noted, our Christology is retrospective. Our affirmations of faith are made by looking back to the Jesus of history, his life and his message. Our conclusions of fact are relative, and our conclusions of faith are confessional. Both John's image of the preexistent Word and our faith in the risen Christ (the post-Easter Jesus) are dependent on the Jesus of history.

Consequently, the emphasis should be on humanity rather than, though not exclusive of, divinity, with the understanding that our image of the *historical Jesus* has already undergone some interpretive shaping. So we maintain the humility of relativity, and we stay confessional rather than coercive.

Guidelines for future Christological dialogue should include these five considerations:

1) A Christology for the 21st century will be dynamic rather than static. It will be evolving rather than frozen in any one worldview or cultural expression. As we have seen, there has historically been a tendency toward rigidity.

This does not mean that our Christologies can be separated from their roots in the Jesus of history. But often fruits look different from roots, and how "the old, old story" impacts "the new, new moment" may be a little surprising.

And it will be important to maintain humility and a sense of our finite relativity as we affirm certain metaphors over others.

Oden, for instance, in his book *After Modernity . . . What?* derides "process theology" as a "fadism" that deabsolutized and debased Christian language but that was, in turn, unable to deliver its own utopia. I would hold that "deabsolutizing" is needed from time to time in a multicultural, multi-faith environment in order to encourage and sustain dialogue and should not be assumed to be a *debasing* process.

It may be that Oden expected more from "process theology" than the process theologians themselves expected. In fact, much of Oden's book seems to be a kind of dissociation from all the disappointing fads to which he had devoted himself too wholeheartedly. Most philosophical, psychological and theological *fads* are only intended as spectacles or metaphors in terms of which one explores "the Way." They usually are not understood by their proponents as "the Way" nor as the ultimate destination. Process theology did not intend to deliver a utopia.

The problem with a static orthodoxy is that it freezes the interpretive process and seems to suffer from a failure of nerve in the ongoing quest for encountering God. One reason for staying in the past for one's *orthodox* perimeters may be the fear that we will not meet God out there in the future.

But Jesus himself seems to have been *process-oriented* and a *contextualist*. Several scriptural illustrations come to mind. His handling of the scriptures in itself shows that for him the accepted wisdom from the past was not immutable. Witness the emphasis in the Sermon on the Mount, and the number of times Matthew quotes Jesus saying, "You have heard that it was said of old but I say to you." Or again, Jesus' words, "The sabbath was made for man, not man for the sabbath" (Mark 2:27), show that Jesus was not bound by an old legalism, and that the context of a given situation might alter one's perspective and actions.

Remember Craddock's comment in *Overhearing the Gospel*, "Jesus can command one candidate for discipleship to leave all other responsibilities and instruct another to sit down first and count the cost" (p. 67-68). A prescription for one person may not be what another needs. To be true a precept does not have to be universal.

Jesus' own approach to life, scriptural interpretation and psychology of dealing with people seems to have been dynamic and flexible rather than frozen and rigid. So our Christological formulations should, in their form, reflect the kind of person Jesus was.

2) A Christology for the 21st century will be incarnational rather than equational. The distinction I want to draw here is to affirm with Paul that "God was IN Christ" without then concluding that

God and Christ, or God and Jesus, are one and the same.

"Theandric man" language and the one-dimensional tone of the early church councils are too mathematical, lacking the warmth of the ongoing human story. Whether intended or not, it is too easily understood as equational rather than incarnational.

Incarnational language is first a category for theology before it is a category for Christology, suggesting how God is active in the world. God is known through his activity in the world–whether through the person of Jesus, the Holy Spirit or the particularity of numerous individual lives. This is, perhaps, a broader than usual definition of "incarnation," but I understand incarnation to mean especially, but not exclusively, the *infleshment* of God in Jesus. It carries the sense that in an unknown variety of ways God is *with us*.

Gardner Taylor, preaching at Marquand Chapel at Yale Divinity School in 1976 spoke of incarnation as, "The *long* (italics mine) record of a bruised and anguished and determined love that will not give up . . . not even by the tears of a Jeremiah or the lyricism of an Isaiah could he get to us . . . until by entering our time sphere, becoming death eligible . . . we knew he could get to us because he had got with us . . . calling us to be participants in the sweet-sad music of the affairs of humanity . . . Our high, holy and hazardous calling."

I admire the poetic warmth and the descriptive powers that emerge out of the tradition of black preaching. My only caution in this instance would be to suggest that God may, in fact, have gotten to or with some through "the tears of a Jeremiah or the lyricism of an Isaiah." Even Jesus himself may have felt God's presence through the emotions and the poetry of the Hebrew prophets. These may possibly have been some of the channels by way of which God's intentionality became present in Jesus Christ, part of the process of incarnation.

113

Preaching in that same Beecher series four years later William
Sloan Coffin, Jr., identified Jesus as "God's love *in person* (italics mine) on earth." For Coffin the freedom to act, to extend, to
serve is what God's love gives to mankind in the person of Jesus
Christ. He is careful, however, not to say these gifts are given
ONLY through Jesus Christ, but that Christians see themselves
especially in Jesus. And because we see God relating creatively
and lovingly to us in Jesus, we know that we should so relate to
one another–a sort of infinite extension of the incarnation.

What else can it mean to call the church "the Body of Christ"
unless we understand it signifies that the church is to carry the
awesome responsibility of continuing to *inflesh* God in the world?

3) A Christology for the 21st century must reflect the larger
purposes of God and will therefore be inclusive rather than exclusive, invitational rather than authoritarian. Once again
"Theandric language" and creedal language like *true God of true
God* tend to be triumphalist and exclusive, and therefore, coun-
terproductive to the cause of Christ.

For me the two key texts for defining the "cause of Christ, the
larger purposes of God," are John 3:17, "For God sent the Son
into the world, not to condemn the world, but that the world might
be saved through him." And 2 Corinthians 5:19 reads, "God was
in Christ reconciling the world to himself."

Our Christological affirmations must not, by their language or
metaphorical insularity, tend to rule out those who do not share
our cultural or religious heritage. Our beliefs, our language and
our approach to others should leave room for the grandness of
God and space for God to reach others in ways we may not have
suspected.

In the same Beecher lectures in 1980 Coffin said, "If our personal beliefs about what is right and wrong separate us from our

fellow human beings, then there must be something wrong with what we believe . . . The integrity of love is always more important than the purity of dogma."

What this means for Christological formulations–past, present and future–is that when our understanding of the purposes of God comes into conflict with our doctrines (belief systems) about God, doctrine must bend to purpose. If our human formulations of what we believe God is like (ontological metaphors) conflict with our convictions about what God wants, then it must be that our ontological metaphors are not yet quite on target. Remember Jesus' words in Matthew 7:21. "Not every one who says to me, 'Lord, Lord' . . . but he who does the will of my Father."

So, in a world of different faith orientations where wise, sincere and seeking people in different cultures coexist, we as Christians must shape our language about our beliefs in such a way as to be inclusive. This is not to say that "what we believe doesn't matter," but our beliefs should be large enough to help us find and celebrate the common ground with people of other traditions. It is vital that Christian language not tend to leverage non-Christians on the basis of "we know something you don't know." We must be confessional and not coercive, invitational and not combative.

Rabbi Marc Gellman and Msgr. Thomas Hartman make the point this way in their book *How Do You Spell God?*, "All religions teach us to help people whenever we can. . . . All religions teach us to play fair and not to hit or kill or steal or cheat. All religions teach us we should be forgiving and cut people some slack when they mess up, because someday we will mess up too. All religions teach us to love our families, to respect our parents and to make new families when we grow up. Religions all over the world teach the same right way to live" (p. 6-7).

And our Christology must be inclusive rather than exclusive, not only for the sake of dialogue with the larger world in which we live and which God loves, but also to protect us from being one-dimensional in our understanding of God or Jesus.

A little fuller attention to several positive images suggested by William Muehl and Marcus Borg will set the stage for a brief critique of the doctrine of substitutionary atonement and clarify Jesus' role in the salvation story.

In his book *Why Preach? Why Listen?*, Muehl expressed his concern that we not "make God a prisoner of the incarnation" (p.85). Certainly Muehl's theology is incarnational, but not *exclusively* so. His metaphor for incarnation is carried in the following anecdote:

"One December afternoon many years ago a group of parents stood in the lobby of a nursery school waiting to pick up their children after the last pre-Christmas session. As the youngsters ran from their lockers, each one carried in his or her hands the 'surprise,' the brightly wrapped package on which the class had been working for weeks.

One small boy, trying to run, put on his coat, and wave to his parents all at the same time, slipped and fell. The 'surprise' flew from his grasp and landed on the tile floor with an obvious ceramic crash.

The child's first reaction was one of stunned silence. But then he set up an inconsolable wail. His father, thinking to minimize the incident and comfort the boy, patted his head and murmured, 'Now that's all right. It really doesn't matter, son. It doesn't matter at all.'

But the child's mother, somewhat wiser in such situations, dropped to her knees on the floor, swept the boy into her arms and said, 'Oh, but it does matter. It matters a great deal.' And she wept with her son.

> The redeeming God in whom we hope is not the parent
> who dismisses our lives with a pat on the head and mur-
> mured assurances that they do not really matter in cosmic
> terms. It is, rather, one who falls to the earth beside us,
> picks up our torn and bleeding spirits, and says, 'Oh, but
> it does matter. It matters eternally'" (p. 92).

Now this story with its affirmation of "incarnation theology" has
greater impact because of Muehl's cautions about the dangers of
preaching about God in only one dimension (God as Redeemer).
For Muehl it is vital that we also speak of God as Creator and
Judge. Without judgment, for instance, how can we know the
requirements, the responsibilities that loving entails. Says Muehl,
"The preoccupation of preaching with God's redemptive love (as
seen in the incarnation) . . . has corrosive consequences. It has
tended in various ways to confuse people about the nature of
love itself" (p. 61).

His point is that love without ingredients of judgment and creative responsibility dehumanizes. "Those," he says, "whom we
do not blame we do not regard as responsible. Those whom we
do not regard as responsible we do not see as fully human. And
those whom we do not see as fully human we are willing to twist
and manipulate to suit our own convenience" (p. 65). And surely
that is not loving. And is not Jesus' own *lovingness* more responsible, more real, when seen as the action of a real human being
and not a Godman?

The problem, as Muehl frames it, is how to preach redemption
without robbing day-to-day life of its meaning. The problem, as
I see it, is how to preach redemption without robbing Jesus' life
of its meaning. The most helpful way to do that is to maintain
our focus on Jesus' humanity, with which we can more fully identify.

Muehl is a powerful spokesman for the incarnational understanding of God, but only in the inclusive context of a creative and judging God who also continues to be wrapped in awesome mystery. Again, *incarnational* should not be understood as *equational*–that becomes exclusive.

Another perspective on the importance of an inclusive Christology is presented by Marcus Borg in *Meeting Jesus Again for the First Time* when he elaborates on what he calls the three "macro-stories" of the Bible (p. 119-136).

They are the stories of the Exodus and the Exile, and the third is not a story as such, but the institution of the temple, priesthood and sacrifice in ancient Israel.

He says that these macro-stories shaped the religious imagination and life of ancient Israel and the early Christian movement. The stories, each in their own way, image what the religious life is most centrally about. Each claims that there is something wrong with our lives as we typically live them, and each speaks of a solution to the problem. Each offers a diagnosis of the human condition and a cure.

The Exodus story, central to Israel's self-understanding and to Israel's sense of relationship to God, is a story of bondage and liberation, a story of journey and a destination.

The Exile story emerged out of the historical experience of the Babylonian captivity when, following the fall of Jerusalem in 587 B.C., the Jewish survivors were marched into captivity, removed from home and tradition. It was an experience of separation from all that was familiar, secure and precious. It is a story of estrangement and alienation and, eventually, a journey of return.

Both the Exodus and Exile stories are salvation stories, and in the New Testament Jesus is, at times, presented as Savior in terms of these stories. In Matthew, for instance, he is the new Moses who leads us out of bondage, his teachings (including the "new law") and the example of his life help us on our journey. In John's Gospel he is *the way*, *the good shepherd* who leads his sheep.

The "priestly story," based on the institution of the temple, priesthood and sacrifice, presents a different kind of salvation agenda. The *priest* is one who makes us right with God. This story portrays the human condition as *sinful*. We are sinners who have broken God's laws. "Seen through the lens of this story," says Borg, "the religious life becomes a story of sin, guilt and forgiveness" (p.127).

The priestly story has become the primary lens through which the church has interpreted the meaning of Christ's life, but Borg sees some major problems with it. One of his primary critiques is that "though the priestly story speaks of God as gracious, it places the grace of God within a system of requirements . . . Moreoever," he says, "this story is very hard to believe. The notion that God's only son came to this planet to offer his life as a sacrifice for the sins of the world, and that God could not forgive us without that having happened, and that we are saved by believing this story, is simply incredible" (p.131). Taken literally, I, too, have trouble with the image of Jesus that the priestly story portrays.

My conviction is that Jesus was not raised because he was perfect, but because he lived seriously and joyfully and with faith in God.

Incalculable harm has been done to our understanding of Jesus and to what is implied about God by the theory of "substitutionary atonement"–that we are saved by believing in the sacrificial death of the perfect *Son of God*. To the contrary we are *saved* (made whole, renewed, accepted and affirmed by God) when we associate ourselves by faith (trust, dependence, acceptance, attitudes, actions) with the life of one who was himself faithful (whose dependence was fully on God). We are saved, not by Jesus' perfection, but by God's grace which we experience most clearly and most powerfully through the faithfulness, preaching and teaching of Jesus Christ.

That is what Paul means when he says that we are saved by faith and not works–i.e., Jesus' faith and our faith being like his–believing in and seeking to live out the manner of his relationship to God. If it is necessary that Jesus was perfect, then we would be saved by works.

Jesus was not raised because he was God's son but because of the quality of his faith and his dependence on God. If resurrection were his birthright as the biological "Son of God," how can we relate to that?

Bishop Spong's candid critique of so-called "substitutionary atonement" is appropriate here:

> "To speak of a Father God so enraged by human evil that he requires propitiation for our sins that we cannot pay and thus demands the death of the divine-human son as a guilt offering is a ludicrous idea to our century. The sacrificial concept that focuses on the saving blood of Jesus that somehow washes me clean, so popular in evangelical and fundamentalist circles, is by and large repugnant to us today. This understanding of the divine-human relationship violates both our understanding of God and our knowledge of human life" (p. 234, *Rescuing the Bible from Fundamentalism*).

Gil Bailie in his recent book *Violence Unveiled* points to the theory of substitutionary atonement as "logically incoherent" and "morally and theologically inadequate as well" (p. 37). Discussing the suffering Servant Songs of second Isaiah as providing clues to the early Christians for understanding the meaning of the crucifixion, Bailie makes it clear that the implications of sacrificial atonement found in these Servant Songs (the idea of placating divine wrath, for instance) are not in harmony with the character of God revealed by Jesus' life and death.

He says, "as beneficiaries of gospel revelation, we are now better able to distinguish the New Testament revelation from its sacrificial antecedents, and . . . we have a responsibility to do so" (p. 46).

I find it satisfying that a similar critique was spoken 190 years ago by Barton W. Stone, one of the founders of my own denomination, the Christian Church (Disciples of Christ).

Stone said in his *Autobiography* (p. 56), "In 1804 my mind became embarrassed on the doctrine of the atonement." The alternatives as he saw them were between Calvinism and Universalism, depending on whether Christ died only for the elect or for all men. Stone found the flaw in this false dilemma. He said that it could not be true that Christ had paid to God, on behalf of either all human beings or the elect only, the debt and penalty incurred by sin. For, he contended, if a debt is paid by a surety or guarantor, it is *paid*, and no grace or forgiveness is needed from the creditor. Such a legalistic system would make the grace of God of no effect. Further, he reasoned, justice is not satisfied by the punishment of an innocent person in place of a guilty one.

Stone concluded that the whole doctrine of substitutionary atonement is contrary to reason, scripture and civil law and has no legitimate place in religion.

So we do not want to be exclusive in our Christological metaphors by limiting ourselves to only one of the scriptural macrostories. And certainly we do not want to be restricted to the one

121

against which Jesus himself was the most vocal; that is, the institution of temple, priest and sacrifice, where intermediaries hold the reigns over our relationship with God. In fact, in the New Testament the priestly story is meaningful partly because Jesus subverts it, giving forgiveness without the *institution*. His message is clear. God loves us just as we are without our having to earn it by fulfilling a new set of requirements.

Indeed, there are moments when certain ingredients of the priestly story are helpful in interpreting the meaning of Jesus' life and the divine-human relationship. Sometimes we are separated from God by sin and guilt and do need the relief and release of forgiveness. But sin is not the only thing that separates us from God. What if, for instance, Moses had gone into Egypt and said to the Hebrew slaves, "My children, your sins are forgiven." They would probably have said, "What? What does that have to do with us? We need to be liberated from slavery, not have our sins forgiven."

Thus, each of the stories speaks to some aspect of the human condition, and Borg concludes, "For some, the need is liberation; for others, the need is homecoming; and for still others, the need is acceptance. But beneath their differences the stories all image the Christian life as journey whose central quality is a deepening and transforming relationship with God" (p. 133).

The problem for Christianity arose when the misinterpreted application of the priestly story became the almost exclusive lens through which Jesus was seen as savior, distorting that story into the legalism of substitutionary atonement.

It is in this context that some attention should be given to questions such as, *How is Jesus' death redemptive?* and *Did Jesus have to die on the cross?*

If not as a price paid to defray the wrath of God, what is the meaning of Jesus' death?

It is my affirmation that the meaning of Jesus' death must be set in the context of Jesus' life. For instance, which is more important, that Jesus lived or that he died? And that question can only be answered in the light of *how* he lived and *how* he died.

We remember that the scriptures tell us not so much what Jesus thought about himself but what the Gospel writers and Paul wanted us to think about him. But surely the scriptures provide hints as to what Jesus thought of himself.

I believe that the scriptural case can be made that Jesus felt some messianic identity in the broad context of the Hebrew tradition. He would not have thought of "Messiah" as being *the same as* or *equal to* God.

He felt and demonstrated by his teachings and prayer life a special closeness to God and he felt anointed or called to the task of reinstituting the reign and rule of God in people's lives.

His death is meaningful and redemptive because the stance and style of his life were meaningful and redemptive. Words from the cross like "Father, forgive" and "Into thy hands I commit my spirit" are presaged in his teachings and the manner and manners of his living.

Without the Beatitudes in Matthew 5, the Lord's Prayer in Matthew 6, Jesus' response to the woman caught in adultery in John 8, the story of the Good Samaritan in Luke 10 and the story of the prodigal in Luke 15 we would have no context within which to understand or claim redemptive power in his dying.

What if Jesus were physically and genetically the son of God but had not lived in harmony with and in support of the purposes of God? Would his death have been meaningful and redemptive?

123

The answer, of course, is "no."

His death is meaningful in a number of ways but all are related to the manner and message of his life.

   a)   His death demonstrates his conviction that the purposes of God are stronger than the death of one person. Surely we see that he could have negotiated "a deal" with the authorities, but he refused to deny the ministry and message to which he had dedicated his life. His death says, "Here is how a godly man accepts the mockery of the crowd."

   b)   The godly response to violence is not more violence. He rebuked Peter for taking up the sword and he would not rally the crowd into a frenzied army.

   c)   Gil Bailie in *Violence Unveiled* says, "By acclaiming the victim as Lord, the Gospels slowly begin to awaken an empathy for victims everywhere" (p. 27). He affirms that empathy for victims is Christianity's cardinal virtue and believes that the crucifixion announces the eventual death of scapegoatism violence as an option of social machinery.

   d)   Jesus' death has meaning given to it by the growing positive response of the disciples. Their eventual affirmation of his resurrection, their dedication to his purposes and the growth of the church against all odds became the announcement that death could not hold the Son of God.

The Bible is clear in affirming a distinction between Jesus and God. Illustrative texts are Mark 10:18, John 14:28, Philippians 2:5-9, John 3:16-17, Matthew 7:21 and Luke 12:10. Few texts can be set over against these–perhaps only John 1:1 and that is subject to broad interpretation.

The Bible is clear in affirming Jesus' sonship. Cogent texts are Romans 1:4, Mark 1:10-11, Matthew 1 and 2, Luke 1 and 2 and John's prologue.

But the Bible is not so clear in dealing with the issue of sacrificial atonement as part of the meaning of Jesus' death on the cross. Many texts emphasize it: 2 Corinthians 5:21, Hebrews 9:22, 1 Peter 2:24, 1 John 4:10, to name a few. Texts from the Hebrew scriptures such as Leviticus 17:11 and Isaiah 53:4-5 provide some of the background in which the early church found interpretive clues for understanding Jesus' death on the cross. It is in the light of such texts that Bailie says Christians have the responsibility to separate its message from these sacrificial antecedents.

But even the Hebrew scriptures are not one-dimensional in providing antecedents that endorse the idea of sacrificial atonement or of a God who would want such a thing. As early as Genesis 22 in the story of Abraham's willingness to sacrifice Isaac, the angel of the Lord stays his hand. The sacrificial death of a human being is not what God wants. That is not what God is like.

And there are a number of New Testament texts that do not emphasize sacrificial atonement. Some like 2 Corinthians 5:19-20 mix the metaphor ("God was in Christ reconciling the world to himself" is non-sacrificial while 2 Corinthians 5:21, "For our sake he made him to be sin . . . so that in him we might become the righteousness of God" has sacrificial overtones). Others, like Matthew 7:21, Mark 10:21 and Philippians 2:12-13, put the emphasis more on quality of life, loyalty and sincere seeking.

I do believe that Jesus gave himself sacrificially for our sakes, but not in the sense of making a "blood sacrifice" of himself to appease the wrath of God. How he lived and what he lived for led to his death, and he was willing to "pay that price" that the world might understand what he stood for. This is related to the continuing, creative activity of God in bringing order out of disordered confusion, in bringing light out of the darkness.

As quoted in an earlier context, "no poem is written, no picture painted, no music made, no sinner forgiven, no child born, no man loved, no truth known . . . except grace took a risk, bore a burden, absorbed the evil and suffered the pain" (Miller, *The Dilemma of Modern Belief,* p. 57-58).

I have given extra space to these considerations because it is just on such an issue that we must practice our interpretive responsibilities, asking how the whole reading of the Biblical message influences our understanding of specific parts of it. We seek to bring a growing perspective of what God is like to the separating of wheat and chaff as far as individual texts are concerned.

An exercise in comparing texts can demonstrate the complexity of this issue and how we have sometimes been lured into a one-dimensional misconception of "what we're supposed to believe."

The statements in the left-hand column are excerpts from a recent Lenten sermon by one of America's best known and most respected evangelists, Dr. Billy Graham. The statements in the right-hand column are taken from the New Testament.

I ask the reader to judge. Which statements are most expressive of what God is like?

"There is no spiritual healing apart from Jesus Christ and his death on the cross."	*"Truly I perceive that God shows no partiality, but in every nation any one who fears him and does what is right is acceptable to him."* *(Acts 10:34-35)*
" . . . his death is our only salvation."	*"Not everyone who says to me, Lord, Lord,' shall enter the kingdom of heaven, but he who does the will of my father who is in heaven."* *(Matthew 7:21)*

"We were lost, and Jesus came to die on the cross for us. He was born to die."

"I came that they may have life, and have it more abundantly."
(John 10:10)

It is not inconceivable that Jesus could have been true to his convictions and died in some other manner. He might have been killed by the sword of a soldier while at prayer in the Garden.

That would not have changed the meaning or the redemptive power of his death or his life. It might mean that the Christian symbol of faith would be a sword rather than the cross, but it would not significantly alter the meaning of our faith.

I do not mean this to be offensive. The symbol of the cross is deeply precious. A real historical tragedy and the eventual triumph of a resurrection faith are centered on those crossed pieces of wood. It is perhaps the richest symbol the world has ever known.

I have dallied in historical reconstruction only to emphasize once again that the Christian faith is not based on a foreordained drama in which Jesus was just acting out a role, knowing all along that things would come right in the end. The Christian faith is based on the life of a man who wrestled with real issues of loyalty and morality, who gave himself wholeheartedly into a relationship with God which he allowed to define every aspect of his being. In the context of that relationship he faced the forces of fear, prejudice and injustice and stood against them in the way he believed God would have him to do.

In him we believe we know more what God is like and what God would have us to become. Thanks be to God and to Jesus for their inestimable gift.

A Christology for the 21st century will underscore the larger purposes of God and will be inclusive of all the macro-stories and other scriptural images as well.

4)   I believe that emerging Christological formulations for the 21st century should put the emphasis on the humanity of Jesus rather than stressing so one-dimensionally his divinity.

For almost 2,000 years the emphasis of the church has been toward a *high* Christology in spite of the fact that the witness of *the sense of the scriptures* is more toward a *low* Christology. According to the Pauline hymn in Philippians 2, "Jesus did not count equality with God a thing to be grasped." Then in Mark 10 Jesus said, "Why do you call me good, no one is good but God alone," and even John's Gospel quotes Jesus saying in John 14:28, "for the Father is greater than I."

I reject the formula "Jesus is God" for two reasons: a) Jesus would not claim it for himself; even the disciples reflect that reticence. b) It contributes to the defeat of the purpose of Jesus' life and ministry by creating unnecessary division among those who "respect God and seek what is right" (Acts 10:34), though of different faith persuasions.

Whether intended or not, the language of Nicea encourages a triumphalist attitude and has for many people throughout history put Jesus in place of God, rather than celebrating Jesus as a way to God. This borders on idolatry. I believe Jesus has greater meaning for us as "God's man" rather than as "Godman."

It also seems that the rhetoric of the early church fathers tended to freeze people in a superstitious orientation to their faith that cannot now, in our more scientific age, continue to hold meaning for the masses. As Spong comments in *Born of a Woman*, "the heart cannot finally worship what the mind has already rejected" (p. 176).

Some distinctions and clarifications should be drawn. To speak of Jesus' divinity need not be the same as saying, "Jesus is God." We can affirm Jesus' special, unique relationship with God without that becoming a disqualification of the efficacy of other faiths. We can feel that God is *with us* in a very special and confessional way without *grasping* for Jesus to be equal with God.

But the category of *divinity* need not be abandoned. Metaphorically, it can be used to affirm the specialness and the dignity of Jesus and to draw us as human beings toward our higher potentials. Paul, in Romans 8:22-23, spoke of *the whole creation* and *we ourselves* waiting *for adoption as sons*–suggesting *sons of God* or coming into our own *divinity*.

And, finally, as we have seen earlier, maintaining some distinction between God and Jesus (as in *sender* and *sent* and *begetter* and *begotten*, as in *Father* and *Son*) makes John 3:16-17 a richer affirmation of God's love for humanity. Risking one's son (and having one's son want to bear the risk) in the hope of accomplishing a great purpose is more awesome, a more powerful image, than risking one's self.

5)   A Christology for the 21st century will be universal and not tribal in scope–inclusive of, but larger than the Jesus of history.

The Jesus of history is reported to have pointed beyond himself to the continuing work of God's love let loose in the world. This thrust of God's love is broad and deep, working itself out through spiritual channels larger than our concepts of the historical Jesus, larger than our concepts of the church. It percolated in the seeds of life and light released by the post-Easter Jesus, the resurrected Christ.

When in John 10:16 the Gospel writer has Jesus say, "And I have other sheep, that are not of this fold," he expresses a largeness of purpose that finds greater specification in John 3:17 and 2 Corinthians 5:19, and that may well move beyond the sectarian, denominational or even "Christian" categories shaped by our belief systems.

This emphasis finds expression in a poem entitled "Communion" written by my father, William H. "Bill" Alexander, minister of First Christian Church in Oklahoma City until his untimely death in 1960. He embodied (another word for incarnation) the spirit of a Christology large enough and open enough for centuries to come.

Communion

I met a man last night, a foreign born,
'Til the wee, small hours we plumbed the mind's far ken,
Because the golden flame of friendship burned
He timidly came back again.
We boldly thought and talked of kingdoms great,
Not built on power but braced by love's strong beam;
At last I sense the bond that binds us,
The truth of Tennyson's dream.

His tongue is not my tongue,
His race is alien unto mine; yea, worlds apart,
But in the dreams we dreamed last night,
The brotherhood of man was in the heart.
I've known this man for aeons now it seems,
How could this alchemy so quickly come so true?
He answered when he said, "My friend of old,
The Christ in me salutes the Christ in you."

The life of the historical Jesus and the spirit of the risen Christ, the post-Easter Jesus, have power for a needy world beyond their meaning for the professing Christian.

Just as the image of a creator God can find resonance in the metaphors of other faiths, even so, the redemptive intentionality of

God as we affirm it in Jesus Christ, does have universal application.

Did Jesus live and speak only for those who would stand in his religious/cultural heritage, or was Jesus' message and meaning larger than the Hebrew tribe of Abraham through which two of the gospel writers traced his lineage?

His life, his message and certainly most of the metaphors that describe him and his mission are framed by this Jewish heritage (later modified by the Greek philosophical orientation of the early church fathers). But the *meaning* for us must not be ossified in any one language or world-view. The interpretive process will go on as we seek new metaphors or invest old ones with fresh meaning for our time, so that the redeeming love of God as we have seen it in Jesus Christ may continue to find expression in all the world for all people.

How will that happen? I believe it will happen most effectively if our emerging Christological images are *dynamic,* not stuck or frozen in one historical era, and *incarnational*, emphasizing that God is *with us* in an awesome variety of ways. Of course, some have seen that most especially in Jesus the Christ and thus call themselves *Christians.*

I have tried to demonstrate that a viable Christology for the next century must be *inclusive* and give more emphasis to *Jesus' humanity.* That is, our understanding of the meaning or efficacy of Jesus' life will not be restricted to professing Christians, nor will supernatural images be taken literally. They are metaphorical in intent. Insisting that *Jesus is God* confuses the issue for Christians and non-Christians alike.

Finally, our Christological formulations will be *universal,* rather than tribal, in order to express the comprehensiveness of God's love and grace for all creation.

May our Christ be large enough, yet humble enough, to serve the universal purposes of God! Amen.

→ → ← ←

▒ Toward a Christology for the ▒
21st Century
Chapter Seven Questions for Study and Discussion

1. Why do the New Testament authors use so many different word images to describe who Jesus is?

2. Should "incarnational language" be reserved just for Jesus? Can the church be understood as incarnating godly characteristics? Other individuals?

3. Where did Jesus get his understanding of God? The Hebrew Scriptures? His parents? Was he just born with it? Was there process, learning and growing in his life?

4. Does God love only Christians? Only Americans?

5. Do our daily lives really matter? If I am prejudiced against some group or persons, maybe I was meant to be that way. What do you think?

6. Was the resurrection physical or spiritual? Have you read 1 Corinthians 15:50?

7. Are we "saved" by grace or faith? Read Romans 3:21-31. What about this "expiation by his blood?" Is it possible that, in spite of Genesis 22, Paul still believed in *blood sacrifice* as a way of appeasing God?

8. Could it be that a growing understanding of what God is like, combined with our different world-view, has made Paul's reference to *blood sacrifice* archaic and primitive— even a misrepresentation of God?

→ Don Alexander